*To my daughter, Kaya.
May your light reach far and wide.*

A Mad Desire for God

Karen Tenney

A MAD DESIRE FOR GOD

by Karen Tenney

First Edition

Copyright © 2012 by Karen Tenney

All rights reserved. No part of this publication may be reproduced, distributed, or transmitted in any form or by any means, including photography, recording or other electronic or mechanical methods, without the prior written permission of the publisher, except in the case of brief quotations embodied in critical reviews and certain other noncommercial uses permitted by copyright law.

Please note that Miracle of Love®, Path to Ultimate Freedom®, Center of The Golden One®, GMP® – Gourasana Meditation Practice®, Miracle of Love Intensive®, Path of Two Masters℠, SAC® – Spiritual Advancement Course®, The Intensive®, Ashram of the Master℠, Come into the Light Ashram℠, (all the registered names that are in the book,) are all registered trademarks of Miracle of Love®.

This book consists of the recollections, perspectives and viewpoints of its author Karen Tenney. It is not an official publication nor does it represent the official position, teachings, viewpoints, or necessarily express the views of Center of The Golden One.

Library of Congress Control Number: 2012922161
ISBN: 978-0-9886361-0-1

Printed in the United States of America.

Book cover and interior designed by:
Desirée Luth
DesireeLuth.com

Book layout and typesetting by:
Rochelle Mensidor

Cover lotus photo by:
Bahman Farzad
lotusflowerimages.com

ACKNOWLEDGEMENTS

First, I acknowledge my mother and father who supported this entire project. Without them, this book would not be in your hands. I thank the rest of my family – J.M. for his generous legal and spiritual advice and Kaya for her endless understanding and love.

I can't thank enough my amazing caregivers, Gina Montouri and Sylvia Litchfield. They, along with my best friend, Diana Blue, have shown me such loving kindness, patience and support.

And then there is Joseph Gunnels. This book would not have been written without him. Joseph took what came out of my mouth, raw and uncensored, and brought his mastery with words as well as a spiritual seeker's heart to our partnership. As a friend, he taught me great compassion and patience as I struggled with cancer. His stamina and vision have supported me to see this project through.

Next, I am especially grateful to Marlowe Kayce, who tirelessly and meticulously transcribed every word I spoke in this book and Jayden Inglis, who gave so generously of her time to proofread and copy edit the manuscript. Thanks also to Andra Joyce Higa for her help with transcription. And a special thanks to Ed DeRosis for doing the final proofread of the manuscript.

Then, of course, there is Desirée Luth and the gratitude I feel for her amazing publishing, book-design and marketing expertise.

For giving feedback on the manuscript I must thank Julia Gunnels for adding her sweet magic to the rough draft. Blessings to Kate Zurich, G'Angela Gerilyn, Honey Adler, Darrin Zeer, Gail and Perry Epes, Tamara La Toto and Karen Karpowich for reading the completed text.

Thanks and love also to Catherine Coates and Lara Lyndy for their financial contributions.

All photos and illustrations in this book were provided by Center of the Golden One, Daisy Talleur, Cole Kaplan, J.M. Sandlow, Kate McBride Tenney, Ben Hood, David Casdan, Barbara Whisonant, and Ginny Robinson. My beautiful hibiscus tattoo was created by Adam Rose.

A special thank you to Center of The Golden One (Miracle of Love) for granting me permission to include its many quoted teachings, materials and photographs in this book.

Kalindi with her first disciple, The Lady (1996)

DEDICATION

This book is about my nearly twenty-year-long relationship with my spiritual master, Kalindi La Gourasana (Kalindi to her disciples). It is humbly dedicated to Kalindi's first disciple, The Lady, a living master in her own right. In this lineage, Kalindi was the first disciple of Lord Gourasana, "The Golden One." Lord Gourasana is a current-day Incarnation of God.[1] Neither Kalindi nor Gourasana is still in the body, although their presence is very much alive in their disciples and others who knew them.

Today, The Lady stands before me as a vital example of how to let go, give up and surrender one's very existence to the will of the Lord. With purity of heart, she offers her guidance as Kalindi did before her, so that those who follow her might consciously depart this plane of illusion for good and forever at the natural time of death.

---

[1] According to Gourasana, "an Incarnation means all the love of God and all the power of God is coming in, and the only thing that can be received is love." Gourasana, *The Radical Path Home to God,* Miracle of Love, First Edition, 2008 (p. xii). Other Incarnations before Gourasana include Jesus, Buddha and Krishna.

The Lady in Prayer, 1997

Through Lord Gourasana's presence and 'special assistance'[2] and with Kalindi's and The Lady's guidance, I have fully and lovingly committed myself to the "Path to Ultimate Freedom." From my direct experience, the promise of spiritual freedom made by Lord Gourasana is being fulfilled. I am one of those determined to break the cycle of birth and death in this lifetime.

---

[2] Kalindi tells us, "Due to the unusually large number of souls that want to return Home at this time, this specific spiritual help from Gourasana [has] come explicitly [from God] to help people who are asking to break the cycle of birth and death in this lifetime. This energy started in the 1960's [and today] is available throughout the world." Kalindi, *The Break-Free Message,* Miracle of Love, First Edition, 2008 (pp. xx-xxi)

Breaking Free and Returning Home to God

It is the hardest thing to do in this world, and that is to break completely free from this material illusion and return Home to God.

You cannot make it without special power and assistance from God and a spiritual master that is connected fully to that special power. You must be able to receive critical information to guide you out of the illusion and into the arms of the Lord.

Everyone's path will look different because each person has a different set of circumstances that they must work through and break free of. Though the teachings are for everyone trying to come closer to God or trying to break free, what each person will actually go through will be highly individualized. And in the end, everyone will fully understand and have compassion for each other's endeavor toward Home.

The transformations move in stages from beginning work to intermediate to advanced and to the ultimate: "Lord, I surrender to you. I lay at your feet in humility and love. I only want you."

My Eternal Love,

*Spiritual Master and Voice of God,
Kalindi La Gourasana
June 24, 2003*

CONTENTS

Introduction 3

CHAPTERS

1 – My Early Years 9

2 – Meeting Kalindi 26

3 – Finding the Best Dad for Kaya 37

4 – Finding Devotion and Humility 45

5 – True-Self Manifestation 49

6 – The Ashram of the Master (2006) 58

7 – Letting Go of Illusory Love – Men & Sex 63

8 – For Love of My Daughter 71

9 – Getting Personal with God 83

10 – Getting the News 88

11 – The Come into the Light Ashram (2011) 104

12 – Conscious Departure 117

13 – "It's a Miracle . . ." 139

14 – Conclusion 146

Kalindi La Gourasana – *Ultimate Freedom: Union with God* (p. 7)

INTRODUCTION

This book is about my spiritual journey. It tells of my early life and how I learned to cope and make do. I was one of those children who cried on the inside while presenting a bold face to the world that hid my true feelings of unhappiness and longing. The reason for the unhappiness was easy to trace through my life. The longing was a mystery. I longed for something; I just didn't know what.

This story is about what happened when my life changed during a single nine-day period. It tells of my being drawn onto a spiritual path that I couldn't understand even as I rejoiced in the feelings it brought me. In these pages, I will share how I met Kalindi La Gourasana and she became my spiritual master. I will attempt to relate how, since the day I met her, Kalindi did everything she could to set me freer and freer from material consciousness, with the ultimate goal of breaking me free from the cycle of birth and death in this lifetime.

This is *not* a how-to book nor the story of how a spiritual master works with every disciple. It is a personal account. I am one of several hundred disciples of Kalindi. She intimately worked with each of us one-on-one.

She liked to say she was our 'travel agent,' here to take us Home. She certainly fit that role in my life.

Kalindi was incomparable as a spiritual master and as a person. Soon after I met her, Gourasana declared that Kalindi was 'The Voice of God' and 'Spiritual Master for This World.' At first I thought this claim was utterly grandiose. How could a single person speak for God? Now, after years as her disciple, I have come to experience that what she declared is true. Through her absolute belief in God, I have found my unfolding faith. Over time, I have come to hold Kalindi's and The Lady's guidance as my only hope for breaking free. (The Lady is Kalindi's first disciple.)

Kalindi's utterly unique destiny is described best in her book, *The Break-Free Message*:

> *Kalindi was given the special destiny to personally present spiritual truth to people who want to hear it, as the living Voice of God. As such, she founded the 'Path to Ultimate Freedom' in 1991. Since that time, she has been guiding [those on] this Path and awakening spiritual masters. She has been delivering teachings and programs to help thousands of people to become freer and freer of the illusion each day and to become closer and closer to the endless love of God. This Path is part of Miracle of Love, now referred to as the 'Center of The Golden One.'* [1]

Kalindi died as she lived. Her death came at an utterly unexpected moment. In late February 2010, she flew from Denver to Hawaii to go into seclusion. No one knew that we would never see her again in the flesh. The end came so fast. Nothing could be done. Her organs failed one by one and, just like that, her life was over. Less than twenty-four hours after being admitted into a hospital emergency room, Kalindi La Gourasana peacefully left her body on April 18, 2010. When I heard the news, I was utterly devastated. I didn't know how to go forward without her.

---

[1] From Kalindi's book *The Break-Free Message,* Miracle of Love, 2008 (p.xvi).

Two months after Kalindi departed this earth, I was diagnosed with a malignant brain tumor. Losing Kalindi and being terminally diagnosed sent me into a mad desire for God. I knew there was no time to waste if I was going to let go of every shred of material attachment and illusion separating me from Him. I had to do it now, before it was too late. With Kalindi gone, I felt desperate and discouraged. How could I make it without her 'break-free' guidance? Would I find the strength and courage to keep going? Little did I realize then that the grace of God would manifest through The Lady, this Mission's second Spiritual Master for This World. It was The Lady who re-ignited my desire to never give up, and to keep falling deeper into my longing for Home.

Some of my story may shock or disturb you. Some of it may make you want to judge me. Who could blame you? I judged myself when I chose to follow Kalindi's guidance, even when it appeared to go against my most basic instincts. Regardless of your reaction, it is my prayer that the story of my transformation will assist in making Kalindi's help available to anyone who feels the call to go Home to God in this lifetime, as well as to all who want to carry more love into this world. Both are equally necessary in a world starved for God's Love.

We live in a time of epochal change. Many believe we have entered the end of times as foretold by the prophets. From the Bible to the Tao we are warned: things will get worse before they get better.

Lord Gourasana brought this path and its practices at this time on earth for those both seeking to break free as well as those wishing to get freer and freer. These offerings, one known as the Path to Ultimate Freedom and the other called Freedom Walk, offer humankind a way to calmly navigate day-to-day life and find ultimate union with God. Neither is a belief system. There is no religious dogma, nor blanket process. This spiritual journey is for anyone to travel in his or her own unique way. Anyone from anywhere could become a disciple of Kalindi (or one of the other spiritual masters who took disciples, like The Lady). People from all faiths can use the offerings from Center of the Golden One to move faster spiritually. Kalindi used to say, "There are many paths, but only one God." The altars in each of our communities and Centers embrace all world religions because of Kalindi's respect for and appreciation of every faith's worship of God.

Gourasana came in response to the cry of souls all over the world seeking to draw closer to the One True Source. As always, in answer to the suffering of humanity, God sends a stream of spiritual masters, gurus, avatars, guides and teachers to earth. The more desperate the desire, the more powerful the help sent by The Almighty. Given the anguished suffering of these uncertain times, Gourasana came to walk this earth "with a Heavenly Host of Light Beings whose specific purpose is to bring special assistance for rapid spiritual transformation to the many people who seek full awareness and love of God."[2]

Gourasana also gifted us with a meditation practice that became known as the Gourasana Meditation Practice (GMP), named after Him. It is more publicly called the Modern-Day Meditation practice, designed to help people find inner direction for achieving both spiritual and material success. The meditation has already helped thousands of people relieve themselves of the burden of old habits, concepts and beliefs that cause so many so much unnecessary heartache and separation.

Created by Gourasana in 1994, the Modern-Day Meditation shines new light on the time-honored custom of meditating. It includes all facets of our being: mind, body, emotions and spirit. The Modern-Day Meditation is both simple and direct. It can be used by anyone of sound body and mind.

Designed to calm the mind, senses and emotions, the Modern-Day Meditation helps us to (1) let go of unnecessary suffering and separation, (2) open the heart to receive greater love and truth, and (3) take in practical information that can be put into action in spiritual and material life. The Modern-Day Meditation does not require belief in anything. It teaches us "to listen, say yes, and act" on answers we receive during meditation. It is grounded in the common-sense truth that love

---

[2] From Gourasana's book *The Radical Path Home to God,* Miracle of Love, 2008 (p. xiii).

is a practical and beneficial response to life. Best of all, there is no way to do this meditation incorrectly.

Unlike meditations in which practitioners focus on quieting the mind, the Modern-Day Meditation is an active meditation. It is of benefit in the moment and of inestimable value when part of an ongoing spiritual practice. The Modern-Day Meditation uses all types of music to evoke feelings. Depending solely on the participant's desire, there can be slow or rapid spiritual movement.

The Modern-Day Meditation has four parts:
1. A period to open or release excess stress, feelings and emotions
2. A period to calm the mind and senses
3. A period devoted to meditative thinking in which higher intelligence is accessed and we gain greater clarity and focus
4. A period when we take action in the world based on what has been realized

Sometimes the Modern-Day Meditation brings tears. Sometimes other emotions need to be strongly expressed. Becoming open to the energy of this meditation moves us beyond our minds into the realm of Spirit. Sometimes I get there with no apparent movement at all. At other times, it takes tremendous effort. Gourasana says, "Whatever experience comes to you, welcome it. Let it take you over."

And best of all, no one needs a particular spiritual orientation to practice the Modern-Day Meditation. There are no doctrines taught and no concepts required. The Modern-Day Meditation is Gourasana's benevolent and all-loving gift to the world. It is also the backbone of my spiritual practice.

The Incarnation, Lord Gourasana, "The Golden One"

For me, Gourasana represents God's unconditional Love – a love so deep, powerful and abiding that it will never be forgotten by anyone Gourasana touched.

I physically saw Gourasana at two different events. Each time, I was deeply affected by His presence and the light that poured from His eyes. When I first saw Him, I hardly believed that God existed. In fact, it was a blessing for me that the singular love I felt emanating from this Being did not require belief. What this presence brought forth within me was a deep desire for Home. It came intuitively, emotionally and undeniably. I was being connected to something so much larger than me, and I wanted the connection to continue forever. From that first experience, I could feel that the love He radiated was real and available.

Kalindi

Without understanding why and even before I had a personal relationship with her, I took Kalindi into my heart and she became my spiritual master. This master-disciple relationship only deepened over the next eighteen years. During that time, I would spend weeks on end in close connection with her. In her presence, my beliefs were suspended, my habits changed and my concepts no longer mattered. She taught me how the longing for something more, a longing I had felt all of my life, was my thread Home to the Kingdom of God. She said that this longing was a doorway leading within towards the love I had always tried to find outside myself.

In this book, 'breaking free from the cycle of birth and death,'[3] enlightenment, 'coming Home,' 'returning to Source,' and 'ultimate freedom' are synonymous terms that speak to the soul transcending material form and connecting to Spirit, never again to reincarnate. No rebirth. No more suffering and death. Kalindi claimed that, at this time in human evolution, those who are ready to take this leap in consciousness can return to Source, and in this transformation, bring more of God's love and light into this world for everyone.

---

[3] The cycle of birth and death – reincarnation – is the belief that the soul, upon the death of the body, returns to earth in another body. Not everyone believes in reincarnation. This belief is not necessary to receive benefit from these teachings and practices.

CHAPTER 1

MY EARLY YEARS

I was born in New York City in 1959. That makes me one of the last of the 'baby boomers' and youngest of 'the 60's generation.' I grew up in exciting times. Like many other boomers, I was born with a passion for social change and little or no religious affiliation. Unlike most others, I was also born into wealth. My family owned three homes, hired live-in nannies to take care of my brothers and me, and sent us to the best private schools in Manhattan. As a family, we took yearly trips abroad to places like Nepal, India, different European nations and the Caribbean. Twice we skied in the Alps on winter breaks from school, staying in five-star hotels everywhere we went.

From early on I knew I was privileged to live, travel and experience the world as I did. At the same time and along with millions of others, I also knew I was part of a generation who believed we could make a difference for good in the world. This hunger for change characterized both my years as a teenager and young adulthood and then later in my life as a spiritual seeker. My spiritual path has been all about constant change led by a master who changed so radically from day to day that no one could keep up with her.

How My Parents Met

My parents met in their early twenties having been cast in Arthur Miller's play, "A View from the Bridge," at the Arena Theater in Washington, DC. When the play's run ended, my father was scheduled to go on the road, and he asked my mother to join him. This was his way of proposing. My mother readily agreed to his proposal, both because of her attraction to this strikingly handsome young man and because she wanted to break free of the tradition-bound future her parents had planned for her. My mother's father was overbearing and her mother was compliant to her husband's wishes. He insisted on naming their daughter after his French mistress, "Margot," as the name was spelled in France. Grandma Dorothy complied.

Their daughter was supposed to be a young Jewish lady who should behave within the Jewish tradition, especially when it came to marriage. My father was a goy (non-Jewish) actor. He did not fit the bill. He was not a proper match for their daughter. My grandparents threatened to disown my mother when my parents first married and only later came to accept my father for who he is despite their prejudices.

As theater people, Mom and Dad both rebelled against their upbringing, reveling in living eccentric, bohemian lives. They smoked pot and swam in the nude. They stayed up late with other artists and lived the Big Apple's version of the cutting edge. They also owned a brown and tan Bentley and liked to drive the family around the city, eliciting envious stares from the people crowding the sidewalks. The Bentley came from my mother's side of the family. My dad's ride was a motorcycle. Sometimes he'd take that bike through Manhattan with my mother sitting behind him, my older brother and me sitting in front and our dog, Winnie, in the open lock box on the back.

Mom and Dad in their 20s

My father was born in Mason City, Iowa in 1930. He was the second of two boys. A third brother arrived eight years later. According to my father, his mother was very kind and outrageously independent – she married thirteen times. "That must be some kind of record," I smartly remarked to her one day. She looked at me and remained silent. My grandmother never talked about her past with me or anyone else. My father told me that she married so many times because "she didn't believe in extramarital sex." When I asked my grandmother about this comment, she replied, "That's nobody's business but mine!"

Chapter 1

Grandma Myrtle, my father's mother

Her first husband, Vivian Schmidt, fathered the first two boys. Grandma left him after four years of marriage because he was physically and verbally abusive. This was a trend that carried over into many of my grandmother's future relationships. The one exception was Bill Tenney. Bill Tenney adopted my dad and his brother and treated them as his own. He also fathered a third son, Bobby. The family settled in Los Angeles where my dad attended high school and college before moving to New York City and a life in professional theater.

My dad was twenty-seven years old and my mother twenty-four when my parents got married in 1957. Their first child was Matthew. He came in 1958. I, the only girl in four generations of Tenney boys, was born one year later. Matthew and I bonded because of our proximity in age and because we were both afraid of our mother, who had a history of flying into fits of rage for no apparent reason. Usually her fury would descend on one or the other of us. When it was Matthew's turn, I tried to disappear.

As a general rule, my parents yelled at each other non-stop, flinging nasty epithets back and forth when they fought. I can remember many mornings as a child being awakened by the sound of slamming doors and shrill voices rising up from downstairs.

Sometimes these fights would go on for days. Often they ended only when my father left. When that happened, my mother made no secret about how she felt being left saddled with Matt and me. I was still quite young the first time she told me that she had never wanted kids in the first place and that we "wrecked her career" as an actress. Mom's mood swings had her in her room with the door locked half the day. Matt and I learned to walk silently on tiptoes when passing her room so as not to disturb her. We had no idea at the time that Mom was bipolar.

It wasn't all bad with my parents. There were times of real joy in my childhood. I loved traveling with my mother. We had memorable adventures, traveling by train through Europe when I was eighteen years old and had taken a year off from school. We went to the opera in Vienna and skied in Saint Moritz, where we stayed at the Badrutt's Palace Hotel, a favorite of celebrities and royalty. One night over dinner at the Palace's elegant dining room, we were seated at a table for two. By the end of the evening, another sixteen people had joined us.

My mother is the consummate hostess. She loves inviting people into her life. To this day, she invites others to live with her, particularly theater people. She adores everything about the theater, whether she's performing or in the audience. Even when we traveled, we were always going to the theater. One time we flew to England and saw seven plays in the span of a week. Because my mother and I share a similar sense of humor, we've had a lot of laughs together. My mother is also highly intelligent and well informed. I have always loved being with her when she made herself available to me.

When working on a theater project, my parents' relationship was as good as it ever got. They were doing what they both loved, and a certain kind of calm settled over the house. So long as there was a production in the works, they were content. When the work stopped, they got cabin fever just being around one another. It was then that the explosive struggles would start up, building in frequency and angry confrontation until my dad left, sometimes for days at a time. My father was an alcoholic, and his alcoholism weighed heavily on our family life.

Matthew and I shared a room until I was seven. We were best friends and confidantes and, as siblings close in age often do, we fought like crazy. At bedtime, we sometimes plotted running away from home. When I was thirteen, Matthew did leave. He went off to boarding school and I was left to cope with my irresponsible parents on my own. Having him gone left a big hole in my heart and life, and for awhile I felt totally abandoned.

My brother Matthew and me in 1969

My youngest brother, Jesse, was born on Christmas Day in 1967. I was eight years old. I remember waking up that magical morning so excited that my baby brother would soon be home. From the beginning, Jesse was my best present. I loved taking care of and coddling him. He was absolutely adorable and I was the best older sister imaginable. I even became his surrogate nanny. I babysat him and gave him baths and fed him and put him to bed.

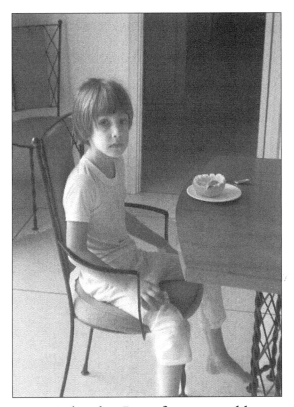

My brother Jesse, four years old

Even so, being 'useful,' or the good surrogate, did not shield me from knowing that something was wrong, something was missing. I could see it in Matthew and Jesse and I could feel it in myself. Was it genetic? Was it part of being human? None of the three of us found it easy to form healthy, intimate relationships. Deep down inside I'd come to the conclusion that I was not good enough to be loved. I seemed to always need more: more love, comfort, safety, and the feeling of being special to someone who mattered to me. My relationships just never seemed to work out the way I hoped they would.

It took many years and much guidance from Kalindi to know that my father was no more capable of safeguarding me than my mother or anyone else was capable of offering the love that I sought. Over time, this knowing has allowed me to forgive my parents for their shortcomings.

In this same way, I've come to understand that my father's alcoholism and womanizing and my mother's belittling and dismissive ways were passed down from generation to generation on both sides of my family. Needless to say and like so many other adults before and since, my father's and mother's parenting skills left a lot to be desired. I learned from a very young age that suffering goes on everywhere. It can be found in every home, every family, and every circumstance known to humankind. My growing awareness of this type of universal suffering has been the cornerstone of my desire to break free.

Still, it has taken more than thirty years to heal that lifelong accumulation of wounds that scarred my heart with mistrust and resentment. In fact, it was only very recently that I permitted 'the child' inside to forgive and love the people in my life unconditionally. It took getting diagnosed with an inoperable brain tumor two years ago for me to realize that it was not worth it to hang on to my illusory judgments that had me bound in all of my relationships.

Throughout my elementary and high school years, my parents were immersed in theater life, with my dad now producing and directing plays as well as low-budget horror films, and no matter what the vehicle, my mother always cast in a role. Sometimes the whole family was cast in one of my father's movies. When I was three years old, I played an extra in "Horror of Party Beach," a flick whose claim to fame is being listed as "One of the Ten Worst Horror Films Ever Made."

Eventually my parents opened a theater of their own in Stamford, Connecticut, where they showcased new plays as well as offered Fairfield County perennial favorites from Tennessee Williams and William Shakespeare. They named it "The Hartman Theater Company." It was subsidized by a foundation my mother and father created to preserve and promote theater arts in America. The theater was their life. To my dismay, it often felt more precious to them than their children.

My brothers and I loved the backstage world of theater. Because my parents blossomed when in performance, it was mostly good times when a show was up and running. And then there were the cast parties. I remember one Thanksgiving when my parents were starring in a holiday extravaganza with a cast of forty. We had a potluck Thanksgiving meal with all the trimmings. The actors were delightful to me. They recited soliloquies from roles they had been in and told funny horror stories about sets falling down and other backstage calamities.

As I grew older, I also learned that the theater attracts some sleazy characters. At age fourteen, I was propositioned by an older, somewhat well known actor who suggested I visit him on the West Coast. I can still remember feeling his hand on my lower back and the smell of vodka on his breath.

About this same time, my experiences with boys my own age were starting to sour. One after another high-school girlfriend confided in me that they had been date-raped. I knew the boys who did it and steered clear of them. Whenever they approached, I walked away. I was particularly struck that none of them showed any remorse, just as none of the girls spoke to their parents or other peers about these sexual violations. The boys seemed oblivious and the girls were too ashamed.

Chapter 1

By the time I turned fifteen, I'd come to the conclusion that men were not to be trusted. There were exceptions, of course. There always are. I had a few gay male friends with whom I liked to hang out. Still, for the majority of the male sex I felt nothing but disdain. Given this state of things, between seventeen and twenty-three, I considered myself a lesbian.

Being Gay in Manhattan

The first woman with whom I fell deeply in love was seven years my senior. She was a light-skinned black woman who taught physical education at my high school. We both knew the ramifications of a teacher being with an underage student, so we decided to wait until I was eighteen before we could act on our attraction.

I was a precocious child who attended college at Wesleyan University in Connecticut at the age of sixteen. At eighteen, I took time off from school. I traveled and took classes in subjects like auto mechanics that they didn't offer at other city colleges. I also moved into my lover's apartment on the Upper East Side of Manhattan. By then, she had left teaching and passed her law boards. So while I completed my undergraduate studies at Barnard College, she went to law school in New Jersey.

As always during my endless academic career, I busted my butt as a student, getting straight A's and graduating Magna Cum Laude from Barnard in 1981 and UCLA's Business School in 1988. Ever the perfectionist, I was never satisfied with my academic performance even when I came out at the top.

Given my lifestyle, I thought I had arrived. By day, when I wasn't engaged in studying at the library, I spent time advocating 'worthy' causes. I joined with other activists to barricade the dean's office at Columbia University in protest of Columbia's decision to receive funding from the South African diamond miners that exploited their workers. I marched in solidarity with César Chavez, founder of the United Farm Workers that protected the rights of non-union, Latino farm laborers.

At night, my lover and I partied at various lesbian bars in the city. It was the Disco Era and we loved to boogie. Our favorite place to dance was Bonnie & Clyde's in the West Village. This was no bar for the faint-hearted. Everyone got frisked for guns at the door. It was a trip just going to the bathroom. You never knew who might emerge from the next stall, or what their intentions might be. It was a heavy-duty scene with the butchest dykes and the prettiest 'lipstick lesbians.' Somewhere around three in the morning, a gang of us would end up at Mamoon's, eating falafel. It was an exhilarating time and place. Wherever we went, whatever we wanted, there were thousands of gay women in Manhattan and we were among them.

On top of it all, I had my own money. Having money allowed me to do some extravagant things. During college I bought one of my parents' houses in Connecticut and turned it into an inn for gay women. The Falls Village Inn was located about two and one-half hours from the city. My lover and I ran it for three years. We offered a safe haven set in beautiful surroundings. Our lesbian clientele came from all over the world. It was a place for women to hang out, swim in the buff and freely express themselves. We had fifteen guest rooms and two staff – my lover and me. We did everything – from making beds to fixing what was broken. It was a lesbian's dream-come-true.

That is, until one day it dawned on me that I might not be a lesbian after all. How else to explain the sudden urge to experiment with men? Suddenly I couldn't imagine going through life without having a relationship with a man. "What is it like?" I asked myself. I decided to find out. As soon as I announced my intentions, my lover walked out, declaring, "If I ever see you on the street, I'm going to shoot you." Just like that, my first real love affair was over.

Loving Men

I've loved my father with all my heart my entire life, but I could never get as close to him as I wanted. Still, he and Mom were my role models for relationship. I followed in my father's footsteps in many ways. For example, Dad was generous to a fault. This is a characteristic I picked up from him at an early age. It became one of my stock tools when ending relationship. Often, as things wound down between my significant other and me, the opportunity would arise for me to give my soon-to-be 'ex' a valuable gift. Gift-giving somehow assuaged the guilt I almost always felt in leaving.

I also learned from my father how to juggle lovers and lie about it – not one of my most admirable qualities. Still, this kind of behavior gave me a very rich sex life during which I experimented broadly without shame. The only downside came with never knowing the intimacy of a long-term satisfying relationship.

Another trait my father and I shared was having an addictive personality. Throughout the decade of my twenties I was a total 'pot-head.' I also suffered from bulimia, an eating disorder that took me years of therapy to overcome.

As with my dad, I have always loved my mother, even though our relationship is so much more complicated. Though brilliant and funny, my mother's rude and sometimes violent behavior made it very difficult for me to be around her. The older I get, the better I understand that her way of being was shaped by her own unhappy childhood. It took me fourteen years of therapy and becoming a mother myself before I realized that the unhappiness I felt inside was passed down from generation to generation. To my knowledge, it can be traced at least as far back to my maternal grandfather and paternal grandmother. My mother's father, Jesse Hartman, had a mean streak embedded in an extraordinarily generous nature. He was volatile by temperament and sometimes scary to be around, especially for his wife, Dorothy, and daughter, Margot.

Just after they were married, Dorothy made her first meal for her new husband. He sat down, tasted it, got up and threw it out the window. She never cooked for him again.

Meanwhile, on my father's side, there is a history of alcoholism, physical abuse and promiscuity. My father's mother, Myrtle, loved to drink so much that when she died, one of her daughters-in-law put a wine cooler, her favorite alcoholic beverage, in her casket to keep her company. So both parents came by their bad habits honestly. On my mother's side, there was always remorse and apology paid off with expensive jewelry. On my father's side, when it was done, it was over. There were no apologies.

Since childhood, I have been committed to breaking this ancestral chain of addiction and violence. I vowed to myself that I would not treat my child the way I was treated. And I haven't, even though at times I have been subject to uncontrollable anger, harsh judgments and bouts of self-abuse.

This negativity played out most dramatically in my inability to maintain long-term love relations with men or women. Thus a major part of my spiritual practice has been about first uncovering and then letting go of habits that cut me off from others. These prove to be the very same ones that keep me separate from God.

Since early childhood I have been empathetic to other people's pains and sorrows. Because it comes naturally to me to care deeply for others, I have developed a keen sense of what is fair and just in the world. This same empathy led me to do what I could to right what was wrong and most likely allowed me to become a good psychotherapist. It has also schooled me in self-reliance. In all of my efforts, I never turned to anyone else. I always felt I could do it alone. In fact, I had no choice because when adversity came, there was no one else to rely on. Clearly no God cared about me. Money couldn't guard against the suffering inside. It bought soft landings and smoother transitions, but money neither removed my sense of unworthiness nor lessened the loneliness and despair I lived with most of my life.

Finding God

One day, when I was in the eighth grade I rode a city bus uptown sitting next to a captivating young Indian woman from New Delhi. We talked non-stop. She told me how she became an American citizen in order to study at one of our universities. She explained that she had had to leave her entire family behind and practically everything she owned, including her dowry. I asked her to come to my school to talk about the life she had endured as an immigrant. Although she spoke of loneliness and separation, she also had this positive and holy outlook that deeply attracted me. I believe our meeting on that bus marked the beginning of my search for God.

Neither of my parents had a real connection to religion or spirituality. My father had been born and raised Catholic but was put off by the hypocrisy he found. He remembered priests who were sexual predators and nuns whose regular practice was to smack knuckles with wooden rulers whenever a student broke rules, was forgetful or needed real or assumed correction. Like most people we knew, my father was proud of his lack of faith. He liked to say he was an atheist. And I suppose he was until he decided to become sober at age seventy. Now as an active member of AA, he readily admits to having a spiritual path based on the Twelve-Step program.

My mother was raised by wealthy Jewish parents who practiced what I call 'social Judaism.' Her family went to synagogue because such customs allowed them to stay connected to other Jews of similar economic and social status. It was a way to find suitable, i.e. Jewish, wives and husbands for their sons and daughters. To put it bluntly, they considered themselves among the high-class Chosen Ones.

Dorothy and Jesse Hartman, my mother's parents

I was very curious about religion throughout my young life. By age ten, I had scoped out the churches nearest my apartment on 82nd and Park Avenue and visited many of them. I loved sitting in the front pews nearest the altars. I'd kneel on the soft cushions and practice what I thought might be somebody's prayer. I loved the smell of incense that permeated the air. I even took communion once in a Catholic Church because I wanted to hear what the priest said as he offered the wafer and wine. I also liked going to synagogue with my grandparents. There was a community feeling among the people who attended. They belonged and I did too. Even so, I never learned anything official about the tenets and beliefs of Judaism or Catholicism. All I knew was that something was missing. There was a deep longing in me to find some kind of fulfillment.

Sometimes I felt so miserable in my unnamed spiritual hunger that I would go to my special 'holy' place behind one of our country homes to cry to some undefined Spirit, begging for a different life and a different feeling about myself. Back then I thought there must be someone somewhere who lived in a normal world that had to be better than what I knew.

Until I met my spiritual master, Kalindi La Gourasana, I think I carried this unarticulated desire to know God, if there was one, in every aspect of my life. I believe this is what drove me to move to the West Coast, first to Los Angeles and later to San Francisco, to study psychology at the California Institute of Integral Studies (CIIS), the only PhD program I could find in the country with a spiritual foundation.

Graduation from UCLA Business School, 1988

I wanted to help others, and there was so much to learn that would expose me to new possibilities. By the time I started at CIIS, I was also signing up for workshops that promised to bring me closer to the truth, whatever that was. Short of backpacking across India, I soaked up the teachings of Eastern masters from Ramanamaharshi to Yogananda. I was drawn to all they said, yet somehow their teachings never quite formulated into a practice for me. I never felt myself at ease with Eastern philosophy. I was not seeking enlightenment. I wanted to understand truth beyond what I'd found in books. I wanted something beyond the intellectual and theoretical. At the same time, I had no desire to step from behind the wall I built to protect me from the pain I'd lived with all my life.

Neither therapy nor workshops yielded the type of movement and lasting change I was looking for. No matter how many sessions with psychologists and psychiatrists, no matter the promises of self-proclaimed gurus, nothing healed the pain. I just seemed to bleed inside and had little to no trust in God or other human beings.

When I got introduced to Miracle of Love in 1993, I had just broken up with my boyfriend of five years. We had moved from New York to California together. I was attending graduate school and he came along for the ride. It was a messy break-up, the kind that left me wondering why I even tried. Nothing lasted. In the end, all I ever felt was bad about myself.

Then I did the Miracle of Love Intensive and found a personal connection with God, a connection that I didn't even know I was missing. Something very special happened for me in the room during that Intensive. Even when I had no idea what I was doing, I worked my ass off to peel back layers of ego in an effort to unburden myself. Little did I know that by the end of those nine days my true self in God would be revealed. What happened for me is not easy to name or describe, but it was palpable. That nine-day event truly changed the direction of my life forever. It opened up a whole new world where God became real and the possibility of breaking free from the suffering was introduced to me for the first time. I felt new and whole. Most importantly, I had found my spiritual master.

CHAPTER 2

MEETING KALINDI

Darshan with Kalindi, 1997

I first met Kalindi La Gourasana (known to her followers as Kalindi G. or Kalindi) at an introduction to the Miracle of Love Intensive in April 1993. The introduction was held at the Howard Johnson's Motel in Mill Valley, California, an unlikely place to hold an event offering a 'God course' led by a spiritual master, as my friend described it. I had done many workshops and different forms of therapy over the years but had never come across one focusing on God. Even before I arrived, I knew that something extraordinary was happening in those Intensives. How else was I to explain my friend's dramatic change?

At the introduction, I was eager to hear Kalindi talk about how this life-altering Intensive might affect someone like me. I listened closely when she shared about people finding an ever-deeper connection to God. I had no idea what she meant by that.

Even if I didn't understand, my mind was intrigued, and from the moment I arrived, I was physically drawn to Kalindi herself. I couldn't take my eyes off of her. In fact, I was so struck by her that I was afraid to get too near and preferred staying in the background to watch as she connected with others.

Some people cried when she spoke to them. Others sat forward as though mesmerized. A number were former disciples of Osho.[1] One told me later that when Kalindi spoke with him, she urged him to "just trust once more." She referred to how some of the followers of Osho lost trust because his path did not deliver as promised. Another person was assured by Kalindi that he could make it in this lifetime. I got close

---

[1] Osho (1931–1990) Formerly known as Bhagwan Shree Rajneesh, Osho was an Indian mystic and outspoken critic of organized religion. His teachings focused on meditation, awareness, love, courage and humor. Deported from the US for immigration violations in the early 1980s, Osho returned to India and died in 1990 at the age of fifty-eight. Today his followers can be found around the world and are referred to as 'sannyasins.'

enough to hear her say, "It takes giving yourself to God completely with no holding back."

What could that mean for me?

Even though I had little idea what I was getting into, that same day I registered for the next Intensive. It started in a week.

The Intensive: God's Kiss on My Forehead

Kalindi led my first Intensive. As soon as I was seated, the opening talk began. Kalindi spoke words of pure truth. I say "pure" because I recognized them as universal truth. What she said could not be denied, and amazingly, it did not seem to require belief.

Even though I had seen Kalindi just the week before, she had changed. Everything about her was magnified. She emanated this larger-than-life persona. Now it was my turn to be mesmerized. Kalindi was beautiful, strong, humble, sexy, and innocent all at the same time. I had never seen anyone so real, compassionate and intuitive. It was as if she could reach inside me and cradle my heart with her words of love. She had such understanding of my predicament. She seemed to be this way with everyone.

And then there was the way she dressed. Given my background, I am not easily floored by outrageous behavior and attire, but Kalindi wowed me. She was so wild and free. I was awed, inspired, and completely carried away. All she had to do was come within twenty feet of me for me to feel surrounded by her presence. And when she spoke, her wisdom seemed infinite.

During this Intensive, we had small-group rounds of sharing. As person after person got up, it became clear that everyone's life was filled with suffering, no matter their background or circumstance. After rounds of sharing, we had long meditations during which we dove into whatever feelings were stirred up.

Kalindi in her outrageous beauty

Every time we meditated, I went deeper. I went through myriad feelings, some of them bottled up from long ago and others that seemed to come from nowhere. I felt a weight come off and a different kind of seeing happening. At the end, I found what Kalindi called my "first baby connection with God."

In that 'baby connection,' I temporarily broke free of my judgments and negative thinking that had plagued me all my life. The fear, suspicion, guilt, shame, and anger were suspended and I was able to feel the light of God within me.

I felt exuberant. I danced in the glory of this connection. I danced and danced until finally I was carried away beyond words into God.

Chapter 2   KAREN TENNEY

May 16, 1998

My dear beloved Kalindi,

I don't know what I would do without The Intensive in my life. It is the one place where I know the illusion does not stand a chance against God's pull. Sometimes I think I would not make it against the illusion if not for this opportunity to give selflessly for 9 solid days and to be in the presence of The Lady, who moves me so deeply and so profoundly towards truth month after precious month. She is God's kiss on my forehead, reminding me that, through the pains and torments of life, there is a benevolent force meticulously guiding us home.

Thanks for never giving up on us and for your loving support.

Karen

My letter to Kalindi, May 16, 1998

In my very first Intensive, I experienced the living force of Kalindi's energy. The best I've ever heard this energy described came recently. One of Kalindi's closest disciples said, "[It is] God's energy, God's movement, the Shakti energy [of the divine feminine] that never dissipates, never sleeps."

That Intensive was the most exciting and amazing event of my entire life. In it, my passion was reawakened and my love for myself and for others was ignited. My thirst for spiritual truth became stronger than any other desire. This desire only grew stronger as I learned to use the tools that continue to propel me forward spiritually.

In that nine-day Intensive, I realized I could never do anything about the past or the future, but right now in this present, I could know God and move closer to Him. This was my first taste of that connection and has since become my personal barometer for spiritual movement. I was given the choice to make changes that were deep and abiding. Kalindi told me I could move as fast as my consciousness allowed. I learned there is no time to waste and that procrastination, wallowing, and denial are all tools of the ego. I learned that my feelings of longing and the emptiness inside I could not fill were God's way of beckoning me ever closer to Him.

It didn't take long before I was 'staffing' as a volunteer at The Intensive. Staffing became part of my life. Being able to serve in such a spiritually alive event started to mean everything to me. Years passed in this way. Thousands of people came from all over the world to attend these events. I was one of the people there to support them as they made their own personal connection to God.

Beginning to end, putting on an Intensive took ten full days.[2] Intensives were scheduled every five weeks. Between participants and staff, there

---

[2] The Intensive has since become a three-and-a-half day offering at Centers around the world.

were often over one hundred people in the room, with half of the staff coming full-time.

It was only years later that I realized how fortunate I had been to participate in an Intensive led by Kalindi. By the end of 1993, The Lady had begun leading the Intensives. For the next ten years, this foundational offering of Miracle of Love was her domain.

Dad and me, August 2011

My dad has always been supportive no matter what I choose to do in life. He trusts me in everything, even though that trust was put to the test by my commitments to Miracle of Love. In fact, it didn't take long for Dad to realize there was something unnervingly different about my involvement in this practice. From the time I brought Gourasana's and Kalindi's teachings to my parents, my father's response ranged from feigned interest to boredom, while my mother's settled on outright hostility. After a few years, I gave up hoping that they or any other relative would ever participate in an Intensive.

Then one day in 2000, I sat my father down and played Kalindi's "Grand Illusion"[3] talk for him. Dad had been sober for exactly one year. This marked the first time he'd heard Kalindi's voice. I don't know why I chose that day or that talk. What Kalindi says is particularly heavy. It focuses on denial around death. In my opinion, it is one of the most serious talks Kalindi ever made.

When the talk ended, my father said, "I've always wondered if there is a God. I'd like to know for sure before I die." He reached out his hand to take mine and told me, "I think I'd like to attend The Intensive." He signed up that day.

I felt so much joy knowing that at the age of 70 my father would finally get a taste of what I had been experiencing. By the time The Intensive ended, Dad shared that his perspective on everything had changed. It gave him a sense of great peace knowing that God is real.

Only one other member of my family has had this experience. In 2009, my sister-in-law Kate decided to participate in an Intensive offered in Asheville, North Carolina. She too found a greater connection with God and herself.

---

[3] The 'illusion' refers to the material realm or that plane of existence of which the earth is a part. It also refers to the actual force of darkness that works against the light of God in the world. Kalindi, in *The Break-Free Message* (p. xix), states that the 'Grand Illusion' universally keeps us in denial about the inevitability of death.

Kate and me, August 2011

During my first years with Miracle of Love, I led a dual life. I continued on as a full-time graduate student in San Francisco and every five weeks flew down to San Diego to staff. It was not until 1997 that I finally left the Bay Area, relocating to San Diego to complete my final internship toward a PhD in Clinical Psychology. Soon thereafter, I quit graduate school. I decided that the whole field of psychology, no matter its spiritual underpinnings, did not carry my soul anywhere. I became even more involved with the Mission,[4] committing myself to this Path, and in my heart taking Kalindi as my master.

I knew from the beginning that Kalindi gave extreme guidance. She knew it is not easy to sever our ties to ego and material attachments. When she took me on as her disciple, she became involved in every aspect of my life. She guided me every step of the way as I sought first to

---

[4] The 'Mission' refers to the fulfillment of Gourasana's main purpose of breaking thousands free from the cycle of birth and death and bringing the love of God to this world.

Also sometimes used to refer to the organization founded by Gourasana to help bring His Mission to reality.

face and then break free of unnecessary or harmful habits, concepts and beliefs that held my personality and 'separate will'[5] in place.

I knew Kalindi was powerful, but it wasn't until the summer of 1994 that she personally touched me with the power of her spiritual presence. My first one-on-one experience of her illustrates Kalindi's unique way of working with each disciple. It happened on a typical day in my life. I had no inkling that something extraordinary was about to occur.

I was headed into a business meeting in the house behind which Kalindi lived in a cottage. I arrived a little early and began conversing with others in the room. That was when she came in. Kalindi got out of her bath, wrapped herself in a towel and, dripping wet, walked out of the cottage, into the house and into that room. She came over to me and said something like, "You need to know you are being called by God. It's time for you to jump. Right here! Right now!!" I had no idea what she was talking about. Her energy was focused on me and my mind was completely blown.

She insisted that, if Jesus Christ had been standing in front of me, I'd be on my knees crawling after Him. I began to sob uncontrollably. Then she said, "This is what true feelings look like," and she urged me to review the next month's Intensive. After that she left the room, leaving just as suddenly as she had entered. It was both shocking and magnificent to be on the receiving end of such audacious guidance.

Kalindi said that each soul comes in contact with an Incarnation when that soul is ready to leave this plane of illusion. As always, when she spoke, her words burned into me. She praised all Incarnations that came before, saying that each blesses those with whom they come in contact. She taught that, just like Jesus, Buddha, Krishna and other Incarnations, Lord Gourasana came in response to the call of this age bringing gifts

---

[5] 'Separate will' is what seemingly separates us from God. It comes in the form of judgments and negative thinking as well as religious dogmas. No matter the depth of our denial, we are never truly separate from God. He loves us always.

necessary to this time, including the blessing of full awareness, or enlightenment, for those seeking it.

I feel so blessed to have received these teachings personally from my master, Kalindi. Her presence in my life increased my desire to share her teachings with others. Because of Kalindi, I know that every part of life can be lived in conscious awareness. She used her own life as an example of trust and faith in God's will. She made tangible the impossible. She believed no price was too high, no sacrifice too great to achieve full union with the Divine.

My soul was connected to Kalindi because it was my soul's desire that she sever every attachment I have to this place. What I found when following her guidance was always better than what I left behind. Even today, all I have to do is practice her teachings to feel the light of God shining through me.

CHAPTER 3

FINDING THE BEST DAD FOR KAYA

When I moved to San Diego in December 1997, all I could think about was having a child. My biological clock was on its last tick-tock. I didn't have a boyfriend, but I knew if I were ever going to conceive, it would have to be soon and with someone on the same path as myself. Because I did not want to marry, my relationship with this man must be of a special nature, 'predestined by God,' shall we say. I had the feeling that I would identify my future child's father right away, and he would be a one-of-a-kind person.

It was at a Fourth of July party when I rubbed shoulders with J.M. Sandlow. J.M. and I had met before. We'd staffed Intensives and attended the same Mission-wide Retreats for five years, but we'd never really spoken. From a distance, he appeared slightly aloof. Still I sensed an attraction and, being a proactive woman, I asked him if he wanted to get together the very next day. He readily agreed. July 5, 1998 marked our first date.

Chapter 3

What a strange date it was. I was working at a residential treatment facility for the seriously mentally disturbed. J.M. and I had barely started off before I got a call from a former patient with Multiple-Personality Disorder. She reported that she had been kidnapped by a man in the vicinity of the facility. I checked and learned she was officially missing. With J.M. in tow, I spent most of our first date looking for her while he gallantly drove me around in his convertible Miata. Three days later, she turned up having escaped her kidnapper. Some lives are so tragic. Less than a year later, she committed suicide.

Partly because of that night, my interest in J.M. was sparked. I was both drawn to his chivalry and fascinated that I'd met a man who was my intellectual match. As well, I was impressed with his emotional depth and down-to-earth nature. Somehow I knew we were connected beyond these bodies, even though from the start we frequently disagreed. These disagreements flared into arguments and then into fights after Kaya, our child, was born.

On the physical side of things, I thought J.M. was endearing, with his scruffy beard and soulful eyes, even though from the start I was never passionately drawn to him. Of equal importance, I was aware that J.M. was deeply connected to God and had a personal relationship with Gourasana. As Kalindi put it, "J.M. was one of Gourasana's disciples." So even though I sensed we might not have an easy time of it, I was utterly certain that he was 'the one' to father my child.

Kalindi also had plans for J.M. to be a spiritual master, someone capable of taking others into spiritual freedom. Kalindi mapped out a destiny for him that – at times – he had trouble accepting. Though J.M. always respected Kalindi as his spiritual master and a powerful teacher, he had difficulty receiving everything she said as 'The Voice of God.' He felt he could ultimately surrender only to God directly.

J.M. and me at a friend's wedding, Thanksgiving Day 1998

I personally witnessed J.M.'s internal battles after receiving Kalindi's guidance. Sometimes, to my surprise, he declined to follow specific guidance. No matter what, Kalindi and J.M. worked it out. She would reiterate what Gourasana used to say around guidance, "There is nothing that is not open to discussion." Because of J.M.'s love for Kalindi and his direct and personal connection to Gourasana and His teachings, he maintained this close and special relationship with her right to the end.

J.M. is an attorney. Kalindi called him her 'pit bull.' She said she could feel J.M.'s devotion as he stood at her side to legally protect the Mission. Before she passed, Kalindi made it clear to her other leaders that J.M. spoke for her when it came to legal matters.

I believe it was on our first date that I confessed my desire to have a child with him. Basically, J.M.'s response was to laugh. He said fathering a child was not in the cards. He believed what he'd been taught when he was a follower of Osho, that parenting would slow him down spiritually. When Kalindi got wind of this belief, she encouraged him even more to become a father. She said it would enhance his ability to break free and that he "would experience a lot of love with this child."

For the next year we dated, becoming more intimately involved with one another. And then J.M. made up his mind. He said he was ready. We agreed to have a baby. We also agreed to not get legally married.

When Kalindi learned of our decision, she called me. It was in the spring of 1999. I remember the moment as clearly as if it were yesterday. I was preparing to go into meditation. I spoke with Kalindi from the pay phone in the hallway of the church. She asked me, "Is he the one?" When I said, "Yes," she asked if I planned to stay with him. When I said, "No," she told me that we would be an example of parenting a child in which the loving parents do not remain a couple. There was a long pause. Then, Kalindi strongly suggested that I not allow strife into our relationship.

If only I had listened, so much heartache and unnecessary suffering might have been averted. But I didn't and neither did J.M. Our history of strife has been very disturbing for everyone involved, including Kaya. Finally, as I face my death, ending this strife has become a conscious and active part of my spiritual practice.

In February 2000, with Kalindi presiding, J.M. and I committed to one another in our own special rite of spiritual matrimony. Love grew between us. From the outset we shared a common desire to create and maintain a devoted and nurturing environment for our anticipated child. As well, we both brought our own concepts and beliefs of what this marriage meant to us. I had judgments, including a belief that a 'good mother' stays with the father for the sake of the child. After all, my parents stayed together even though they fought like cats and dogs. Personally, I couldn't shake the sense of guilt I felt when considering the idea of having a child with someone I knew I wouldn't stay with. This guilt of mine became the cause of much relationship strife over the course of our years together.

Kalindi became intimately involved. She told us what type of toys to buy, what kind of school our baby should attend, and how we should avoid spoiling the child. She even named the baby, but then after two miscarriages, when I was six months along in my third pregnancy, she relented, saying she wanted us to have "the happiness of naming [our] own child."

Kalindi called herself a 'no-shit master.' She demonstrated this again and again. For example, during my third pregnancy she told J.M. he should move out of the house and not come to the birth. J.M. was pretty upset. Nevertheless he graciously moved out and followed the guidance in an effort to let go of his separate will. During this time, he reviewed The Intensive four times and had great spiritual movement. Kalindi could see how much he had progressed spiritually from her guidance and consequently told him he could move back into the house with me. It was in June 2000, four months before Kaya was born.

When Kaya was born, J.M. and I were overcome by our tender love for her. He cried when he saw her for the first time. Many of the photos taken at her birth show J.M. beaming with love and pride with tears streaming down his face. As I lay there, I knew that everything that happened was meant to be, and I was so grateful to J.M. for saying yes. From rubbing my feet every single day of my pregnancy to holding our baby in his arms, I knew I couldn't have found a better dad for Kaya.

Chapter 3

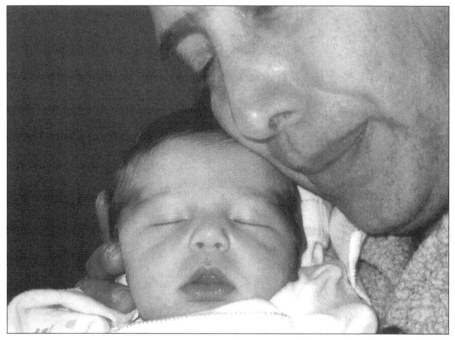

J.M. holding Kaya at 8 days old

Less than a year after Kaya was born, in 2001, Kalindi gave J.M. guidance that physically separated him from Kaya, guidance that she would only have given to someone who wanted to break all attachments to the material realm. He was to see his daughter only on Sundays. Otherwise, they were to have no contact. This went on for five months. When Kalindi did not rescind her guidance, J.M. put his foot down. From that day forward, he swore to let no one stand between him and his child.

As I think back over the fifteen-plus years of our relationship, I realize that J.M. has been a good friend and a great father. When I have been called away, he has willingly shouldered more than his share of responsibility. Even when he declared, "I didn't sign on for this. I never wanted to be a single dad," I have known that he would do anything to safeguard and love our daughter.

Kaya and J.M. hiking in Rocky Mountain National Park, 2011

Since being diagnosed with cancer, I have more deeply recognized the wisdom of my choice of J.M. and have no doubt that Kaya will have everything she needs in a spiritual and material sense as long as her father is alive. This knowing brings me great peace of heart and mind.

One of the great gifts of this illness has been the continued healing between J. M. and me in areas that brought strife in times past. I am so very grateful to God for giving us the chance to be friends, just as I am grateful that He sent me such a clear signal for how He wanted motherhood to be for me with J.M. as my partner. In all of this, we both feel so utterly blessed to have such an incredibly aware and sensitive child who is living proof of His love and mercy for each of us.

CHAPTER 4

Finding Devotion and Humility

You need to become an offering to God,

An offering.

Become an offering.

Place yourself at the holy feet of God,

Like a rose bush without thorns.

And as you surrender and give your life and soul to Him,

More and more the flowers of the love in your heart

Will keep blooming and wrap around God.

Just wrap around God,

Eternal flowers.

Kalindi La Gourasana, June 8, 1996

From the beginning of my transformation, there have been several key areas that needed focused work. It did not take great insight to realize that by adulthood I'd become a collection of habits and beliefs most of which no longer served me. Still, like most others, I'd come to believe that these behaviors were 'me' rather than the by-products of my silver-spoon upbringing coupled with my fair share of adversity and misfortune.

Like so many others, I had a fear lurking down deep inside that seemed to lie at the root of it all. One part of me got fed by a lifelong sense of entitlement and arrogance; another got expressed through my unsettling lack of worth, telling me that I deserved exactly what I got.

In September 2004, at a barbeque to which Kalindi also invited J.M. and Christoph (my husband-to-be), she gave me personal guidance that addressed both my arrogance and unworthiness. She said the program was very strict. She called it *Maha Prasad*, which translates from Sanskrit as preparing an offering of food to God first.

What follows is the sign I made based on Kalindi's point-by-point guidance:

Maha Prasad

- *Prepare food as an offering to The Lord.*
- *Prepare it in full devotion to The Lord without tasting it.*
- *Prepare it from scratch.*
- *Play church music while preparing the food.*
- *Do not let anyone taste the food before offering it first to God.*
- *Place the prepared food on a plate chosen for this purpose solely.*
- *Place the food on your altar as an offering to The Lord.*
- *Kneel down and place your forehead on your hands (palms down, one on top of the other).*
- *Pray to the Almighty offering Him the Prasad.*
- *Once the Prasad has been offered, you can eat.*

- *This food will have a special taste.*
- *Only eat food that is prepared and offered in this way.*
- *You will experience greater worthiness through this devotion.*

I strictly followed the *Maha Prasad* guidance for two years.

The timing and perfection of this practice were uncanny. Not only did I learn worthiness through devotion, but I also learned how to cook, something not taught to me in my youth. Throughout college and graduate school, I cooked only when absolutely necessary, and lived mostly on yams heated in the microwave with lots of butter and vanilla yogurt slathered on top. In the majority of my relationships, we either ate out or my partner made the meal. Me, I just didn't cook.

When I started the practice of *Maha Prasad*, I was living with Christoph. He is an amazing cook. At first I hoped he would teach me. My mouth used to water when listening to stories from his childhood of "cooking with Grandma." From early childhood, Christoph was fascinated by the smells and tastes emanating from his Oma's kitchen. He followed her around, hungry to learn everything about cooking and baking. His own style is very spontaneous. Christoph does not use standard recipes. He puts 'a little of this' and 'a lot of that' into every one of his dishes – whatever enhanced the taste and presentation.

Although his meals are delectable, Christoph is a terrible teacher. It didn't take long for me give up getting cooking lessons from him. Instead, I hired a dear friend to show me how to put together some basic but delicious meals. To this day, I still have the recipes she compiled in a cookbook that resides in every house I've lived in since.

Kalindi promised that by practicing *Maha Prasad* I would "no longer feel guilty about food and how [I] eat." She told me this without knowing that I had been plagued by bulimia. Using her guidance, I eliminated the need to punish myself – the emotional root of my eating disorder. In the course of a single lunch hour, Kalindi opened the door to both personal healing and spiritual growth. With incredible precision she offered me a tool to unravel parts of my personality that I'd spent years addressing with one after another psychologist.

This guidance provided a profound teaching in humility. I literally prostrated myself in submission to God before every meal I ate. At the same time, I gave up one of my favorite social pastimes and pleasures: going out to restaurants. From an early age, I have frequented some of the finest restaurants in the world. I loved being served as much as I disliked cooking. So *Maha Prasad* was a full-on attack against the ego. Besides, it was so humbling to admit that I had to start from scratch in the kitchen at the age of forty-five.

Back then I always made sure there was company to share the food with. More recently, I have discovered that being alone and in silence while eating is not an austerity but rather a time to honor and be with my beloved Lord. *Maha Prasad* taught me of the joy that comes when seeking to please God. The prayers I now lift up around food have become a foundational part of my spiritual path.

CHAPTER 5

TRUE-SELF MANIFESTATION

I was one of a group of disciples who gathered with Kalindi in Hawaii in 1999. There were ten women involved. Over the next two months Kalindi brought in many teachings, one of which was the teaching on 'True-Self manifestation.'

It began when Kalindi asked us to ship every piece of clothing we owned – underwear, accessories, and shoes – to Hawaii. When our wardrobes arrived, she put them in a single pile and said something like, "Okay, we're starting from scratch. It is time to put together a 'true-self' wardrobe for each of you." The shock went through me that I was letting go of all my favorite clothes. And then, I let go.

No one had a mirror. Kalindi wanted us to feel our true selves without reflection. It was a feeling she wished to give us, a sense of beauty beyond this world. Immediately I knew what she meant. I sensed this kind of beauty when I looked at Kalindi.

When I first came to Miracle of Love, I dressed either like a tomboy or upscale and expensive. I was New York chic and looked good in it.

Chapter 5

Everything I owned was stylish and sharp and I owned a lot of clothes. I was used to buying whatever I wanted regardless of price. My wardrobe included high-end, glitzy gowns and fancy lingerie. We're talking about $400 cocktail dresses that showed off my legs and the finest cashmere sweaters to keep me warm. So it was very radical for me to see my designer wardrobe in a pile filled with things that came 'off the rack,' so to speak.

By 1999, I had come to trust Kalindi even when I didn't understand what was going on. She had always told me I would have enough, that there was a greater abundance unlike any I'd experienced thus far.

Still, getting beyond that first shocking moment in Hawaii took a great deal of trust and faith. I had one of the nicest wardrobes in the entire Mission. It represented a lot of who I thought I was. My fashion statement was distinct and form fitting. I liked that 'me' in the mirror. So it was exciting and scary to let my wardrobe go, not to mention way outside my comfort zone.

Poor J.M.! He's the one I called in the middle of the night. He could hardly believe I was asking him to pack up my belongings and ship them to me. When I insisted that he include every article of clothing from my closet and drawers whether or not it made sense, I thought he was going to pitch a fit. But he didn't. Somehow he knew this was what needed to happen. Just like he realized later on that he didn't have a single say in the matter. When it came to outrageous requests from this woman in his life, J.M. trusted and supported Kalindi as well as what I needed for my transformation.

Kalindi wanted so much for every one of us. She had such a vision of who we are beyond concepts of self and beauty. What she saw for me was fundamentally different from anything in my wardrobe. Kalindi put me into these long, strappy negligee-type dresses and nightgowns. Everything she put me in was soft and draped. Kalindi even put floppy-brimmed hats on my head! I suddenly felt very different – very feminine and vulnerable. I found this innocent quality inside, a truer part of me that lay beneath the cultured and intellectual New Yorker or the tomboy I used to be.

When Kalindi gave guidance to a single disciple, there was this powerful ripple effect. The spiritual benefit imparted to one soon impacted all those nearby. In this way, her guidance spread across the Mission. Kalindi was magical in this way – she could move the whole Mission just by moving one of us.

This time in Hawaii was my first major 'let go' in the early years of my transformation. Kalindi took ten women out of our familiar identities and in a few short weeks showed us something entirely new, creating room for something unexpected to happen.

So there I was in this new full-on wardrobe. I was even beginning to like the look. I saw myself through Kalindi's eyes and began to recognize something of what she was doing.

Just when I was coming to see and feel the 'new me,' Kalindi reduced our clothes allowance to a single bin each. My wardrobe shrank from closet-sized to one eighteen-gallon Rubbermaid bin. Everything else was taken away. Kalindi promised that what was packed into that bin would hold all our essentials and that there would be no lack. She helped each of us, hands-on and one-on-one. I came away with one sweat outfit, two shirts, one dress, two pairs of pants . . . you get the idea. Once the bins were full, she told us that these were the only clothes we would wear for an entire year. The only exceptions were for work and staffing Intensives.

As we prepared to return to the mainland, I was more excited by the challenge than afraid to give up my possessions. Still, I wondered: Could I really give up my well-dressed identity? If I did give it up, would I be left with enough clothing? Would I even like the clothing that would end up in my closet?

Secretly I kept reassuring myself, "Kalindi's not going to hold us to this guidance for a whole year. I'll get some of my clothes back." After awhile, I gave up those hopes and for the next year, I lived out of that one bin. In hindsight, I can honestly say I loved the experience if for no other reason than because I really didn't think I could do it. But all ten of us did.

All the clothes we left behind in Hawaii were distributed to the rest of the Mission in what is now known as "Kalindi Mart." Today, Kalindi Mart exists all over the world in every Center and most communities. The whole idea is that somebody seeking change can alter his or her look in a single day without shopping at a store. People are encouraged to donate clothes that don't express them anymore. These clothes are displayed on racks in a central location where community members can come to find something new.

In all things, Kalindi taught us to focus on awareness of what we need. She said, in finding our true self in everything we do, we should have what we need, not too much or too little. And now there was a lot less ego in my clothing choices.

Not only did the clothing exchange break down my ego, it ended a sense of separation and brought with it ecstasy. While still living out of that single bin, I first came to love helping other women find and embody their true-self beauty. It was a joy to see someone light up when dressed in the right outfit that showcased this beauty.

Kalindi explained that the true self cannot come into chaos and disorder. She taught us to organize our wardrobes by color as a way to create a sense of calm and order in our closets that welcomed the true self. It was her wish that her disciples always present our true beauty as a gift to the world and as an act of devotion to God.

Kalindi educated us to recognize that there are always one or two colors that best suit a person at a particular time. She encouraged us to wear these two colors plus black and white. For me it was navy blue and lavender. Limiting myself to these four colors brought a certain order and ease.

When Kalindi first suggested colors and gave me lavender, I shied away from it. Even though it looked great on me, lavender was Kalindi's favorite color. It felt inappropriate for me to wear it too. Only after Kalindi repeated her request did I acquiesce. After all, she was the master and I was the disciple. At the same time, I was regularly wearing white. In white I felt anonymous and unadorned. Navy blue surprised me. I thought I looked stunning in this color. And black has always felt natural to me.

Later on, my colors changed based on my transformation. This too is part of the gift of Kalindi's teachings. By personal example, she taught us that constant change is necessary when letting go of who we think we are. Without change, we remain creatures of habit caught up in repetitive and unconscious ways of being.

Today, lavender reminds me of Kalindi in the flesh. When I wear it, I feel her close to me. I also wear her perfume. I had to smile recently when I remembered that Kalindi once gave me guidance to wear her perfume. She knew the day would come when her fragrance would bring me – and others who knew her signature scent – great comfort.

Kalindi's teachings around true-self manifestation have taught me that in surrender there is always further to go. Perhaps the hardest part of this lesson came when Kalindi gave me guidance to continue wearing white after the 2006 Ashram of the Master.

After four months in the Ashram, I was looking forward to expanding my wardrobe. I wanted to get color back in my life. Instead, Kalindi asked me to stay in white. She did the same with another disciple and then asked the two of us to live together so we could help one another spiritually. Kalindi's main focus was on our vanity. She said this illusion was deeply rooted in both of us.

Kalindi gave us the following guidance:

> *Face your fear on a very deep level. Go deep. Stay deep. Focus continuously moment by moment on feeling the connection to the Lord in your heart and finding Him deep within, leaving all else behind. Let go and trust like never before with the most sincerity that you can find. Don't lose your focus, and don't become distracted [by men]. Break free. Come Home. That's the best thing you can do for [yourself] and for the world. You have to do it now in earnest.*

Kalindi added,

> *You have to feel these words from a different place. Hear Kalindi from a different place, and make each point very separate and very clear. It's imperative for both of you. The world is depending on your finding your depth of love and love of God and compassion born of that love. You have one year to make a drastic change in yourselves, and Kalindi knows you can do it. Desire is everything. Pray to Gourasana.*

In personal guidance to me alone, she said, "Leave all else behind." This simple sentence has played a major role in helping me to find the essence of my prayer to let go of everything but God.

Later, Kalindi gave further guidance to the two of us. She said,

> *The two of you together – pretend that [you are] like Kalindi and The Lady and there is nothing else out there anywhere except Gourasana. And you have to lead . . . and get somewhere. You have a mission . . . and there is no way to do it unless you are filled completely with the Lord. You have to come into the Lord to do what He's asking. You have to find your way now. You have each other.*

On the one hand, she guided us to let go of vanity, and on the other, she asked that we answer the call from God. It was time to stand up and step into the unknown. It was time to recognize that those coming behind were dependent on our letting go. She asked us to let go fast. For me this let-go began with wearing white for as long as Kalindi requested.

I was prepared to face my resistance when unexpectedly it simply fell away. White became an easy sacrifice for me. I grew used to it. I felt at ease. All was going well. Even the vanity in me was starting to fade. Then I was sent to Germany in the middle of the winter.

There couldn't be a less appropriate place to wear white than Munich in the winter. All I had to do was lean against a car or brush against a pile of snow at the curb for streaks of filth to mark my overcoat, shoes, gloves and scarf. I stood out like an oddball. My German neighbors referred to me as "the American in White." At first, I was disturbed. I stood out for all the wrong reasons. Then I lost interest in what people thought and became more comfortable being a fool for God in how I dressed.

My time of wearing white stretched on for three years. During that time, slowly but surely my sense of being special and entitled fell away. White became like a uniform, easy to put on without thinking about making an impression. It helped my true self to become more accessible, real and visible.

Along with wearing white came a practice I chose myself. I turned my living quarters into something of a monastic cell. Everything was functional and reflected God-consciousness. I wore much less makeup and sought out the blessings of a modest life.

The changes I made were both subtle and dramatic. I stopped being lavish. I no longer automatically picked up the tab. There were no more quick getaways with friends. Social interactions no longer filled my calendar. Another wall of that well-made façade I wore came tumbling down.

Even after returning from Germany, I continued to wear white. Then I realized this phase was over. Immediately, I went shopping at Kalindi

Mart and came home with a new wardrobe. This time, I picked out a lot of purples, dark blues, and blacks. White remained in my closet though not on my body. It was there to be looked at. It reminded me of Kalindi.

The 'Anti-Chaos Dress Code'

Before turning away from Kalindi's guidance about true-self expression, I want to touch on a guideline she created called the 'Anti-Chaos Dress Code.' Kalindi explained the purpose of this dress code as follows:

> *As individuals shed the many layers of illusion they are covered in, they simultaneously find the beauty of their true selves. [This] beauty . . . is very simple in its nature. Therefore, it is a teaching [of mine] that people have wardrobes become as simple as possible while still maintaining the feeling of beauty that they are finding within.*
>
> *People must begin to live with every area of their life organized and simplified. Your closet is an easy area to master this practice. By practicing this teaching, people learn that they do not need excess in their lives. They will always have what they need, but they do not have to live with more than what is necessary.*
>
> Kalindi's teaching as expressed by her daughter,
Maha Swanson, July 15, 2005

As noted before, over the years it has given me great pleasure to help others – men, women and children – with their wardrobes. I love being asked to go into other people's closets. It's all about weeding out the old and bringing in the new. The first step I call the sorting process. I ask the other person to try on every single article they own. What doesn't work or is rarely worn is let go. What doesn't fit or is worn out is also cleared away. After that, we fill out the wardrobe with new clothes. Most of these are found at Kalindi Mart. Afterwards, the closet gets sorted by color so that what hangs there expresses a much truer sense of self.

Going through this process is hard for most people. Like me, most start out apprehensive and by the end feel no lack whatsoever. It is self-empowering to consciously know that the clothes we own are the clothes we wear. Even years later, I am reminded by people of the good times we've had in their closets.

I even got to share this teaching with Kaya a year ago when she was ten. I asked her, "Would you like to do something radical together?" Before she could answer, I added, "If you trust me completely, you will be in total ecstasy by the end." She agreed.

One by one, we went through every article of her clothing, including her purses and shoes. I suggested keeping so many items from each category, such as five long-sleeved shirts and three pairs of jeans. Kaya started out crying, saying over and over, "Mommy, this is so hard." I responded, "Keep trusting." She did and by the time we finished, she was laughing in amazement at how uncluttered her wardrobe looked and how good she felt about it. Kaya had really enjoyed herself.

A playful Kalindi dancing in love and ecstasy with God

CHAPTER 6

The Ashram of the Master (2006)

ASHRAM OF THE MASTER
FOUR SIMPLE STEPS

From Kalindi La Gourasana

December 2004

1. *True Humility – Find it and remain in it forever.*

2. *Stay in your depth and connection and do not leave it.*

3. *Constantly Let Go, Give Up, Surrender.*

4. *Desire is Everything.*

The Ashram of the Master is a four-month residential program created by Kalindi. This Ashram is the entry point for people who have advanced on the path far enough along to do the serious work of breaking free. The number one reason to participate in this Ashram is to solidify the bond with God. Each disciple intensifies and deepens his or her connection and trust in Lord Gourasana. By the time a disciple is accepted into this Ashram, most have been on the path for ten years or more. Regardless of our advancement, Kalindi believed that all of us could go further and faster. And she did everything she could to make this happen.

In her guidance for this Ashram in October 2004, Kalindi said,

> *The Ashram is to develop a consciousness of seriousness and a staunch nature. It's to help people give up [what is] binding them and keeping them separate from the pure love of God. It is to help people become truly pure of heart [and] crumble at the feet of the Lord in absolute submission and surrender.*

There are strict prerequisites for acceptance into this Ashram. Foremost among these was Gourasana's teaching:

First, you must be willing to give up your life as you would have it be . . . then you must be willing to live it as God would have it.[6]

Other requirements included:
1. A burning desire for the Lord
2. Self-motivation to break the cycle of birth and death
3. Constant movement toward letting go
4. Being beyond issues and trying to figure things out
5. Control of the being
6. An unalterable connection to Gourasana and acknowledgement of that
7. An acceptance of Kalindi as your spiritual master
8. Following Kalindi's guidance to a 'T'
9. A desire to go Home without doubt, hesitation or resistance

---
[6] Gourasana, *Let Go, Give Up and Surrender, The Gourasana Sign Book,* Miracle of Love, 1998, p. 49.

10. A dissolving sense of separate will
11. A commitment to serve Gourasana's Mission and break free as an example of the Love of God on earth

We were asked to stay in silence as much as possible. By not engaging in social intercourse, going deeper became a habit. Instead of focusing on material matters and issues, the focus became: (1) meditation, (2) contemplation, (3) self-realization, and (4) letting go of binding illusions. For me, the Ashram was welcomed as a 'time off' from the complexity and noise of my daily life and all its distractions.

The Ashram's lifestyle was characterized by a very high level of God-consciousness within and without. We kept the house sparkling clean and set up our environment to be orderly and simple. All distractions were eliminated. Long meditations were a daily part of the spiritual program. Where another time I might have felt confined, I flourished in this consciousness. By the end of those four months, I did not want to leave. And to a great degree, I never did.

Parents who participated in this Ashram found ways to balance fulfilling their Ashram requirements while taking care of the children. I spent most weekdays with Kaya after school from three to five. On Wednesdays, our service night, I stayed with my daughter until she went to bed. Still, it was devastating to her to see me leave and wonder why I didn't spend the night with her.

Because Kalindi wanted J.M. to participate in this same Ashram, he worked out an arrangement to both participate and care for Kaya in the evenings, including sleeping at home each night. J.M. was with Kaya for dinner, then set her up with a baby sitter before coming to attend evening meditations at the Ashram. Late at night, he always returned home to be there when Kaya awoke in the morning.

Between the two of us, Kaya was completely taken care of. And because of our schedules, this became a time when her relationship with her dad grew deeper and sweeter. This time together carried over into the summer. When school let out, they went off on adventures. J.M. and Kaya love to explore. They took many wonderful camping and hiking trips in Colorado. They traveled back East where Kaya spent time bonding with relatives she hardly knew. Through it all, Kaya matured and, as Kalindi promised, she never lacked for anything.

Since early in life, Kaya has had to understand the importance of God in her parents' lives. I suppose she's had few options, given the choices J.M. and I have made. This is not an easy lesson for a child at any age, knowing that mom and dad often put their dedication and pursuit of God ahead of spending family time together.

Those months of the Ashram coincided with the dying of a fellow disciple and very dear friend. She had Stage Four breast cancer. This disciple made a series of videos about her dying process. This brave woman set an example of someone seeking to make it Home in this lifetime. She was the first of Kalindi's close disciples to die. She blazed a trail for how to move with serious intent. Through her, we learned that none of us has the luxury to wait until we are sick and old to find this resolve. We must let go now and give it our all every second of every day. Now that I find myself wearing similar shoes, I know more than ever that it is time to wake up.

Wake up, sleeping souls. Wake up!

Kalindi's Rooster Call to the World, April 23, 2006
(in The Ashram of the Master)

Me in the Ashram of the Master, August 2006

CHAPTER 7

LETTING GO OF ILLUSORY LOVE – MEN & SEX

Illusory love binds you,

Love of God frees you.[1]

Kalindi La Gourasana

I've been 'in love' twice in my life, first with a woman and then with a man. The woman came early in my life. Christoph, the man, came later on. After falling in love with Christoph, I realized there was no comparing loves in life. All love relations are unique. The difference in my life was that Christoph came later when I was a fully-grown woman, ready to experience a deep and mature love. I gave myself to him in every way, and for me, he was the total package. He had it all, including this ability to listen like no other person I'd ever met.

---

[1] Kalindi's teachings about 'illusory love' can be found in her workbook entitled *Illusory Love Binds You, The Love of God Frees You*, Miracle of Love, 1998.

Our relationship started in 2003. As you might imagine, Kalindi set it up. For four years Christoph Strieck had been Kalindi's caregiver. She loved him dearly and wanted him to have a life in which his most fundamental human desires were fulfilled. At the same time, she wanted Christoph to remain at her side as caregiver and traveling companion.

Christoph is the warmest, kindest and most devoted man I know. His love of sensual beauty matches mine. He is very good looking and a great cook and lover. From the beginning to the end of our marriage, when we were together, the world disappeared. I never wanted to be apart from him. Of course, it didn't work out that way.

Kalindi's guidance to all of her disciples included having service for the Mission. She kept me traveling and working on Mission business, just as she kept Christoph on call for her whenever she needed him. All of Kalindi's disciples knew that Mission business was to be a top priority in our lives. So the Mission brought Christoph and me together, and the Mission kept us apart.

In the beginning, Christoph and I lived in a cloud of bliss. It only lasted a few short weeks before he left for Germany as caretaker for Kalindi. She was traveling to his homeland and he had to be at her side. For us, this began an endless round of goodbyes at various airports around the world.

In the beginning, it didn't matter. We were so in love. We learned to fill all of our short times together with meaning. We truly believed our love would overcome anything. It reached a crescendo with Kalindi in the middle of one of those trips to Germany. Christoph told Kalindi he was in love with me and could no longer be 'her man.' I learned later that she cried a few tears, but within a very short time, she completely let go of him. Kalindi never faltered. She always did what God asked of her. Her purpose for everything was clearly and purely united to His will. Still, for Christoph and me, those separations that started so early and seemed to never let up were becoming harder to handle.

Christoph and me at our wedding, January 2, 2006

Later, when they were back in the States, Kalindi suggested we marry. We chose her birthday, January 2, 2006, as our day to share vows in Colorado Springs. We had wedding cake in the morning and Kalindi's birthday cake that evening. Kalindi even sewed by hand the veil I wore. She orchestrated everything.

Our relationship lasted a total of three years during which we spent most of our time apart. After thirty-six months, neither of us could stand it anymore. Still, we shied away from how it felt until I realized that it was up to me to ask the tough questions. I put it to him bluntly, "Do you still want to be in this relationship?" He hemmed and hawed before finally admitting that he was done. Our marriage was over. Bottom line, Christoph said that being apart was too painful when all he wanted was for more of me at his side. He wanted something human, something of the world. He wanted me in a role I could not play.

My deepest desire has always been to give to Kalindi. Even though I was in love with the man she had given to me, I couldn't stay with him if that choice separated me from her. My heart was broken. I couldn't believe that what Christoph and I had together must end. It wasn't supposed to be this way. It felt like we had just started our love affair when suddenly the marriage was over.

As with other disciples, what happened in my personal transformation prompted Kalindi to bring out a series of teachings that are now being offered to the world. In my case, most of these teachings centered on relationship. In this instance, Kalindi addressed my devastation. She knew I was heartbroken. She told me, "Don't for one minute sit in any kind of self-pity." "How to Let Go of a Relationship" became the talk from this phone call between Kalindi and me. In it, she says:

> *You need to let go. . . . You'll never break free if you keep being attached to [illusory love]. Freedom is what you want. Don't give up. . . . Don't [cry] about 'poor me.' Don't go the issue route.*

She went on to share with me about her own personal journey with David Swanson, who was her husband in the time before the energy of Kalindi had come to the earth. Talking about "Carol" back then, she said:

> *[I] was crying [for the loss of my husband when] David said, 'I don't know what you're crying about, but God isn't hearing your prayers or your tears. So you'd better go deeper.'*
>
> Kalindi, "How to Let Go of a Relationship"[2]

Kalindi then shared more of her personal grief, admitting to great pain in many of her own relationships with men. She spoke to her personal experience of how hard it is to let go. She understood that grief is necessary for all of us. It brings us to our knees. It opens the door that takes us to God. Kalindi often said that the only reason we turn to God is because there is no other place to go.

In one relationship, Kalindi admitted that it took six years for her to stop thinking about a man who had left her. She taught me that sorrow is natural and that after awhile, it can become wallowing. She said that wallowing blocks our ability to let go, and letting go of illusory love must take place if achieving ultimate freedom is the goal.

I was ready to let go. It was after Christoph, in February 2008, that I told Kalindi with total certainty that I wanted to break free in this lifetime. This is the first time I had spoken these words out loud to Kalindi. She responded:

> *You've got your road cut out for you. It is going to take a lot of letting go, and a lot of meditating. . . . In India they wear white to symbolize renunciation from the material world – sex, husband, different pleasures. Why don't you take*

---

[2] An unreleased talk from a phone conversation I had with Kalindi on November 7, 2007.

a vow of renunciation for ten years from everything, just as a statement of what you can have with God? [This] is your initiation into a path of renunciation. It is not to shut you down. It's to set you free.

And you can't deny any [feelings or desires].

Celibacy

Through the vow of renunciation, Kalindi was seeking to strike at the core of my illusory being. Her guidance turned out to be a great blessing as well as a shattering blow to who I thought I was as a woman.

I was forty-nine years old when I got this guidance. My first thought was, "Oh, my God, that's it. That's the end of my sex life. I'll be an old lady by the time this phase ends." From where my consciousness resided at the time, Kalindi was asking me to be a nun. Even though I said I was ready to go the distance, her guidance felt horrible – scary and devastating at the same time.

In the spring of 2008, right on the heels of this guidance, I was asked to co-lead a sex workshop. I wept the entire time. Was it even possible to go ten years without a man? I didn't think so! I wanted to take back that 'yes,' but it wasn't mine anymore.

I was sure I was being punished for my years of promiscuous behavior. I'd had so many partners. And where before I felt no shame at all, now I felt nothing but shame. In an instant, my deceptions around sex, all the lying, cheating, and juggling of lovers, turned ugly and cold. And this time the feelings did not fade away. My history around sex suddenly became one of the hardest of my behaviors to look at.

I was in a reckoning with the Lord. There was no way to excuse myself even though I'd grown up in a liberal environment. I had no guilt around sex. I liked it a lot! But then I knew that beneath it all, sex without love had no lasting value and could hurt people, or be no better than a distraction from my path.

Equally, I knew that human love, though temporary, is a precious gift from God. There was no escaping the sense that I should have had a different sexual history. I'd been careless of others' feelings, and now this horrible guidance was my punishment. From free as a bird, I felt such shame and self-judgment.

All I had to do was strip away the pride to see how manipulative I had been in my sexual behaviors. I considered myself to be freer and more advanced than other women because I had taken many sex courses with More University and liked to experiment. I was a free spirit who turned men on. I prided myself in being a male daydream.

My sexual identity defined me more than I knew. At one point in 1999, Kalindi told me that my attention was at least ninety percent directed toward getting a man. It was only after entering celibacy that I woke up to how deeply I desired every man to adore me as if no other female exists.

Celibacy felt less like a choice than any other guidance I've ever been given. It took months just to realize that the act of sex is not as important as the feeling of being desired. Men were there for me because I desired their attention. I wanted them around me in every way. I liked laughing with them. I enjoyed them intellectually, emotionally, and in and out of bed. Male energy balanced me. It was exceedingly hard for me to find that balance being celibate.

Then I remembered Kalindi's warning, "You can't shut down any feelings or desires." I didn't know how I could live in such a state of painful openness. I prayed to God to keep my heart, mind and sexuality open, and as I prayed, I began to receive more of His energy.

Soon my heart softened. I started to interact with others in a new way. It had nothing to do with attraction. My relationships stopped having any undercurrent of sex vibe. I started actively cultivating relationships without desiring to get something out of them.

I started to awaken to the rest of Kalindi's guidance. Where she led me went beyond renouncing sex. It addressed all worldly pleasures to which I was most attached. Once again, I stopped going out to eat or taking weekend breaks. The only time I travelled now was to be with Kalindi. I stepped back from whatever I indulged in. I even stopped going to the movies so regularly.

Taking another cut, abstaining from these pleasures brought me to a new depth. In the midst of these austerities, I began to feel better about myself. The pleasure-seeker was freed up from what she thought she couldn't live without. I became comfortable in a simpler existence. Daily tasks became a joy. Fewer friendships and social interactions led to more time to be with God. Once again, quiet time turned to gold.

Eighteen months after it began, in June 2009, Kalindi sent a message to let me know my guidance of renunciation had ended. She wanted me to change direction. Like nearly everything she did, this news caught me off-guard.

CHAPTER 8

FOR LOVE OF MY DAUGHTER

Love consists not in feeling great things but in having great detachment and in suffering for the Beloved.

The soul that is attached to anything however much good there may be in it, will not arrive at the liberty of divine union. For whether it be a strong wire rope or a slender and delicate thread that holds the bird . . . until the cord be broken the bird cannot fly.

Saint John of the Cross

My daughter, Kaya and me

Where my heart is most attached and my mind most afraid has been around letting go of my daughter. Since her birth, I have been completely in love with my daughter Kaya. Even before her birth, J.M. and I shared our determination to allow Kaya to grow up in a world of safety and security (as if we had any control over this).

I was forty years old the first time I got pregnant. The moment she knew I was pregnant, Kalindi told me to be careful and rest. Based on her guidance, I stayed away from the Mission's San Diego Center. At twelve weeks, I miscarried. It was February 1999.

Immediately afterwards, Kalindi sent me guidance. In it, she said:

> *This [miscarriage] will make you go deep. . . . Before, you couldn't crack into that depth. . . . [Use this time to become] freer, deeper, happier, [more] peaceful . . . [so that] the baby being born won't be disturbed by any illusion in the parents.*

I got to work. Two months later, J.M. and I tried again. This time, I miscarried after the fourth week of pregnancy. After this second miscarriage, Kalindi gave both of us guidance to go deeper to God before trying again.

Nearly a year passed before I once again became pregnant. Healthy and beautiful, Kaya was born October 13, 2000. With her in my arms I felt fulfilled. I loved nursing her and burying my nose in the crevices of her sweet-smelling neck. Every day after her bath I massaged her – for the first year of her life. She was my baby girl.

Kalindi with Kaya, May 19, 2001

Kalindi with Kaya, August 5, 2001

Kalindi met Kaya for the first time when Kaya was eight weeks old. When she first saw Kaya, Kalindi immediately exclaimed, "This will be our first movie star!" She pegged Kaya from the start, knowing somehow that Kaya loves to perform. She always has. Now, at eleven years old, Kaya will break into singing and dancing spontaneously. She also loves to write and tell stories that make me laugh. Kaya also knows how to hold back when she has to. During my illness, she kept so much bottled up inside so as not to disturb me when I didn't feel well.

Facing My Worst Fear as a Mother

Oddly enough, though always maternally proud of my flourishing young daughter, I've often been assailed by bouts of fear concerning her. I feared random mishaps or unexpected events over which I had no control. Given the world we inhabit, some aspect of this fear was quite real. But some of my fears were wholly imagined, no more real than what I found in one of my father's horror movies. At the root of it all, I was afraid that I would have to give up my daughter.

Kalindi knew that on the human plane, where feelings and emotions reign supreme, I am most deeply connected to family and friends. She recognized that what I felt for Kaya was cellular and all-consuming. Anything to do with Kaya touched me fully and deeply.

At the same time, Kalindi knew my faith and connection to her led me to trust. This allowed Kalindi to come down hard on the side of breaking me free from attachments. She finally came to focus on my attachment to Kaya, and I came to face the greatest heartbreak of all. Kaya was so young. It began by Kalindi working with J.M. In order to put God above all else, she gave J.M. guidance to move out of the house and only talk with Kaya by phone once a week on Sundays.

J.M. told Kaya, "I am going into a time of 'retreat' where you won't see me for some time and you will not live with me for awhile." This went on for six weeks. Kaya was bereft without seeing her dad. Then, Kalindi said he could come for Sunday visits. This went on for another five months. It was heartbreaking for us all. During this time, Kaya began to learn the lesson that for her parents, God comes first, even as we do our best to care for her.

I sensed that this guidance to J.M. was a preview for me. Kalindi was preparing the ground. She intended to break me (and Kaya) free of our mother-daughter attachment. She knew of my desire; otherwise, she would never have been so relentless. Without that desire, it might have seemed cruel – and God is not cruel. God does not punish us, as some major religions and fundamentalist sects would have us believe. Even in the depths of my personal despair, I knew God is an all-loving God.

My guidance began when Kaya was four years old. Kalindi asked me to move with Kaya to Colorado Springs, where the Mission was setting up a new community. She asked J.M. to remain in Northern California for five years and continue as spiritual leader of the San Francisco community. J.M. could not agree. He let Kalindi know that "this guidance was just too much." He insisted that I not leave California and take Kaya to Colorado.

Kalindi's spiritual mastery was as flexible as it could be heavy. When J.M. opposed further separation from his daughter, Kalindi turned her focus on me. She asked if I was willing to move without Kaya. My immediate "yes" grew more tentative as time went by. I remember getting the shivers when I learned of Kalindi's mother-daughter plan for us. I was to be with Kaya one week each month. Otherwise, I would not see her at all. The more I realized what I was committing to, the more jarring, traumatic and intense these changes became. I had only to look into Kaya's innocent eyes to feel what it would mean for her to have her mom living elsewhere.

I had to tell her. From the moment she took in what I was saying, Kaya was beside herself with sadness and anger. She couldn't believe that we'd be living in different states for awhile. (I couldn't bring myself to tell her the full extent of the guidance.)

What four-year-old can make sense of her mother leaving voluntarily in order to become closer to God? What kind of mother would choose to do such a thing? I agreed with Kaya. It made no sense to me either, yet it had everything to do with my trusting Kalindi. Kaya wept in my arms and I wept holding her. In late summer 2005, I moved alone to Colorado Springs.

Even though Kalindi never separated loved ones longer than necessary, and then only to fulfill their destiny, I can assure you that trust in one's master does not alleviate the pain. We went through so much sorrow during that separation.

By Christmas, we were together again. This came about when J.M. decided to move early. In coming to Colorado, he had to let go of so much. In order to reunite his family, he left behind his spiritual leadership position, law practice and, ultimately, control over how our family life looked. Within four months of my moving, Kaya and J.M. were living in Colorado Springs. I was overjoyed.

For me, this guidance continues to bear spiritual fruit. I learned to say "yes" to Kalindi, even when it threatened to break up my family and shatter my dreams of motherhood. That's how fully I trusted my master.

In Colorado Springs, J.M. and I lived in separate housing, and Kaya traveled back and forth between us on a fifty-fifty basis. When I decided to move to Denver, J.M. agreed to follow me "one last time." He said, "That's it for us, particularly Kaya. She needs stability in her life." J.M. wanted Kaya to live in a safe community and close to a good school, so he bought a house in Golden, Colorado and declared he was settling down.

My Time in Germany

The second time Kalindi gave me spiritual guidance that separated me from Kaya, she had just turned six. It was October 2006. I committed to co-leading an event in Australia. I had been there for three weeks and was scheduled to return to Colorado in a few days when Kalindi sent a message asking that I go straight to our Center in Munich, Germany and stay there for three months. She was explicit. I was not to come home first. It was time "to get through my fear."

When I received that guidance, I fell to the floor in the bathroom and cried my eyes out. I was devastated. Nothing could be worse or more terrifying for me. Feelings of childhood abandonment drifted in and out of awareness. I was doing to Kaya what had been done to me. Even though mature for her age, she was still too young for me to be away that long. How could I make it okay for her? One again, it was Christmastime, and being together was so special for us at this time of year.

I couldn't rectify any of it. It was summer in Australia and winter in Germany. I had the wrong clothes. I had no desire to go. Even so, within two days, I was making arrangements for winter clothes to be sent from Colorado to Munich – all white, of course. And a few days later, Kalindi was on the phone with me to talk about why I was going. She told me it was time for my heart to melt into His and to heal the pain that was coming with His Love.

How could I heal anything when I ached for my daughter, who was so upset and angered by the news? This was the second time I'd seemingly abandoned her. Kaya was losing faith in me now and I didn't blame her. Unsure that she would ever forgive me for following this guidance, I left it to her father to pick up the pieces of her heart, which as always, he did so tenderly.

Once I got to Germany, I asked a seamstress friend in Munich to teach me how to sew. We spent hours in her kitchen making Christmas stockings, cooking, drinking pear brandy and sewing together a beautiful advent calendar for Kaya. Kaya and I stayed in contact by Skype every morning at 7:00 a.m. Rocky Mountain Time. I tried to make it special each time we talked so she would feel less lonely. Each day she opened an Advent 'pouch' and together we marveled at the little German trinkets inside. Before we got off each call we told each other how much we missed and loved one another. It was a time of such sweet sorrow. And it was when I learned from direct experience one of Kalindi's foundational teachings: 'The longing is the love.'

Each week, I wrote to Kalindi about my spiritual movement. That first week I cried for three days straight before I could even face the fear that caused my tears. Kalindi told me to face these fears on my own. She gave me no instructions. I was left to pray and follow my own inner direction.

As I focused on the fear, rather than freezing up, I felt myself become more fluid and pliable, more willing to relax and able to find a way through without relying on a program. I was on my own. It was up to me whether or not I let anything distract me. I felt no pressure save the ultimate pressure of my own desire to break free. Every day, I wrote in my journal about expectations and beliefs created out of fears engendered long ago during childhood. There I was filled with loneliness and grief as I worked on my childhood while separated from my own daughter.

In congregational numbers, the Munich Center is second in size only to the Home Center in Denver. I lived in a community house with others in the Mission. I had my own bedroom in which I created an area where people could visit. I had candies on the table and served cookies and tea. My guests and I often talked about fears and how these manifested in our lives.

On several occasions, at the request of the main spiritual leader in Munich, the entire community came together and meditated in support of my letting go of fear. I allowed myself to be held by different people as I cried my way through the fear and pain unreconciled from the past.

I jotted down every quote I found on fear in Gourasana's *Breaking the Cycle of Birth and Death*.[3] I put them on index cards and studied them, one by one.

Some examples of what He said and what I learned follow:

Quote #140

> *Do not spend your energy hiding from your fear. Hiding from fear simply perpetuates the problem. Until the fear is dissipated by the light, you must develop greater tolerance so that you can withstand your fear.* (p. 44)

Studying this quote, I asked, "How do I hide from fear?" Slowly it came to me. I rely on false bravado, and when that does not work, I hide behind embarrassment. When all else fails, I adopt a persona that makes people afraid of me. If I begin to feel vulnerable, I hold others off to make sure that I'm not the one who gets hurt.

As these realizations came to me, I took them into meditation. Each time I focused on them, the fear dissipated. Just by shedding light on fear, it disappears. In this state, I came to develop greater tolerance for fear and therefore less need to avoid it.

Quote #175

> *Your fears will have an end. And after you face them, you will look back and say, 'What was it that I was afraid of? There was nothing to fear and yet I was afraid.' You think there is something to be afraid of, but there is nothing to fear. It is just an illusion, no more real than a movie.* (p. 54)

---

[3] Gourasana, *Breaking the Cycle of Birth and Death,* Fourth Edition, 2007.

The movie analogy struck a chord for me. I decided to rent some horror films (my least favorite genre of film). I wanted to see if I could realize Gourasana's words. Could I make the boogey man unreal? Could I let go of the terror that rises up when people jump out at each other to slaughter and maim? Was this fear monster always going to get me? Was I always going to be fatally attracted to fear?

Again, I took these feelings into meditation and found that the boogey man I was waiting for existed solely in my imagination. He lived in my head. I can turn him off and on just like those movies.

Quote #107

> *There will be fear. There will be anxiety. There will be confusion. And it may be uncomfortable. All these states spring from letting go of the illusion.* (p. 34)

This quote teaches me that fear is unavoidable, no matter our path. But that it is there particularly when on a path to freedom. I realized that fear signaled great movement about to happen. It does not necessarily have to be an obstacle to letting go. Instead it can be seen as a doorway or opportunity for letting go.

Quote #29

> *You have created the fear as part of your separateness; indeed, it is the chief ingredient of your separateness. You have created it, and you have the power to uncreate it. You need to know that this is within your power!* (p. 8)

I focused on the words "chief ingredient." I saw that fear is the illusion's last-ditch effort to stop forward movement toward God. So long as there is duality, fear can be found. Fear arises out of the separation that exists in duality. This quote allowed me to own my part and see the role

I play in creating fear. It also helped me to see that I could end it. It is my choice. It is my action. It is that simple.

One of Kalindi's strategies, learned in The Ashram of the Master, had to do with releasing emotions around fear. Screaming works for me. I can scream into a towel as loud as necessary and as long as required, and the fear will disappear. I can also pray.

While in Germany, I traveled by train across Munich, the capital of Bavaria. Munich is located in the Alps and considered one of the most livable cities in the world. It has exceptionally beautiful churches that are open all day. I made a pilgrimage, touring from church to church praying, meditating, crying to God to end my suffering and fear and praising Him for sending me Kalindi.

One completely unexpected fear came up in me when I co-led an Intensive with Germany's top leadership in February 2007. From the outset, I felt over my head. Something was wrong. My energy did not mesh with that in the room. I was spiritually out of sorts and didn't know why. I couldn't get a handle on it. Then it dawned on me. I was not at one with the energy of Gourasana. Fear stood in the way. I could not get to the energy until I let go of the fear. And until I was in the energy, I could not be with Gourasana. Only in this connection could I stand up with authority and presence.

I saw it. I felt it. But I could not act on it. I could not let go of the fear. My mind told me that Gourasana's energy was benevolent, but the fear told me that I could not tolerate the energy. It was too massive, too overwhelming. Even as I begged Gourasana to fill me with His presence, another part of me held back. I could not tear down what blocked my soul from getting through.

While I was in Germany, Kalindi made a talk called "Open Your Heart" (2006) specifically to help people who were abused as children. I became her example of a disciple who couldn't go further without facing that fear. On that talk, she says,

> *I have one disciple that I'm working with right now who has worked very hard on herself but always been afraid. When you look in her eyes, you see the power of God, the truth of God and her seriousness and devotion. But you [also] see that something is missing. There's fear in her eyes, and that satisfying personal connection in her heart isn't there.*
>
> *If you were abused, don't kid yourself. You can't skip over it. [You must] let yourself feel it so that you can get into your personal connection. [The Seminar] is a place where you [will find] help [to] get through to the other side, no matter how painful it is. The Lord will be with you, holding you, whether you know it or not. You can be freed from the burden of carrying that fear anymore. Your heart can be free to love and give love and have love, His love.*

When I returned to the States, Kalindi had me enter a Seminar in which I would not know anyone. I was the first person on the Path to participate in this Seminar. It had been designed for the people new to Miracle of Love work. Kalindi said it was a perfect setting. She guided me to focus on the horrors. She said, "Feel the terror of it all. Forget about everything else. Now is your chance to get to the other side of that fear."

In the Seminar, I had a breakthrough unlike any other. I crossed through the pain and terror buried more than thirty years ago. It was simultaneously intense and exquisite. It was opening a festering wound I thought had healed. I had to muster every bit of courage to come fully into the Light, saying "No" to the illusion. When I did, Gourasana held me and filled me with knowing that everything was all right and truly there was nothing to fear, nothing at all.

Thanks to the grace of Kalindi, I had turned the corner on fear. I now entered a whole new phase. Where before I had struggled in darkness against fear, now I surrendered into His presence and light.

Chapter 9

Getting Personal with God

From the beginning Kalindi said the greatest obstacle anyone will face is fear. I have come to know this as true. Over time, I've identified four great fears: (1) being punished, (2) being rejected, (3) going insane and, worst of all, (4) being taken over by the immensity of God. Being punished, being rejected and going insane all arise out of worldly experience. The fear of being taken over by God feels primal. How can I be drawn to an energy that makes me so apprehensive? I so desired to feel the potent energy of Gourasana, yet I was terrified to give myself completely to this energy. If I let go, my world would surely spin out of control.

Since childhood, I have been well schooled in control, especially around fear. By the time I was in graduate school I was highly educated in dealing with fear. I did it in one of two ways: I either ran away or headlong into it. And because I tended to be recklessly courageous, I usually ran at it with such gusto that I didn't seem to be afraid at all. On the contrary, I loved taking risks. I was a thrill seeker; show me the cliff and I'd walk to the edge, ready to jump.

For me, Miracle of Love was the greatest thrill of all. I dove right in. So in 2001, after eight years on this Path, I was baffled when Kalindi told me that she didn't know if I had opened up all the way to Gourasana's energy. She said I "started and stopped" in my meditations. I went only so far, then put on the brakes.

When she asked if I could feel the difference between those who carried His energy and those who did not, I said, "Yes." I knew I was one of the latter. It came to me in a flash. I'd made this choice at the very beginning. I was the one who stopped my own forward movement because of my fear of 'the energy.'

I remembered experiencing Gourasana's energy in 1993 at my very first Intensive. Right from the start, His energy scared me. It was too far outside my comfort zone. I was much too uncertain when confronted by that massive force. I had a history. My past was riddled with force overcoming trust and faith, particularly in my intimate relationships. If I was not in control, bad things tended to happen. In my imagination, His immense energy not only overwhelmed the mind and senses, it took over control of the entire being in a way I was afraid to let happen.

Because of the depth of my fear, Kalindi guided me to focus on being 'self-motivated.' She told me that this work took a very deep personal commitment. Without such commitment there was only so much Kalindi could do. She said I might have to "rip off the illusion layer after layer with [my] bare hands." She promised that if I let go all the way into His energy, I would find "love and ecstasy beyond my comprehension."

Kalindi taught me to discern between opening up to my connection and allowing the energy to fully enter me. She explained that in opening up, I was still in control. In full surrender to His energy, God was in control. She reassured all of her disciples, including me, that His energy was benevolent but insistent.

I replied, "That's what frightens me." I perceived the energy as being dominating and forceful, and didn't think my nervous system could handle it. She was patient and reminded me to never give up.

In June 2003, ten years after I did my first Intensive, Kalindi told me that even though I was fully connected to God's Love, I still did not carry Gourasana's energy and presence. When I responded how badly I wanted to make this connection, she gave me the following guidance:

> *You need to connect to His personal presence now. You can't connect to yourself without this. [Have] trust and faith that Gourasana is the Almighty Supreme. Want to feel Him. Feel what He feels like. Trust that everything will be fine. Walk away [from the illusion] without knowing what will happen. Once you make that connection, I can take you further. He's the only way out. He is here with so much power. Go to Him. Be completely taken over.*

The moment I said, "Yes," I was so afraid, afraid of the very thing I wanted most of all. From childhood, through dating, friendship and marriages, my heart has been broken again and again. Both men and women have always let me down. I've never felt fulfilled. And yet here I was, ready to say yes to an energy that is beyond the mind and can be felt but not seen.

My brain filled with images of physical and emotional violence from early childhood. Rage and self-hatred intermixed with the fear. I was terrified of what lurked in the shadows and enraged that this was happening to me. All I wanted to do was make the chaos stop. How could I take the chance? How could I open myself up to these feelings? I was certain there was no safety or security in opening up. I was much better off guarding the walls that protected my heart. Once again I chose to shut down rather than let go.

But not for long. . . .

It was in a Seminar in 2007 that my breakthrough came. It began when I opened my heart sufficiently wide to forgive the men in my life – my father, my husbands, my lovers and brothers – for hurting me because they could not be who I wanted them to be.

This opening allowed me to take responsibility for my feelings. Being responsible was a key to letting the walls of my heart finally crumble. I was the only one who could change me. Everyone else involved was beyond my control. They are who they are. How could I blame them for that? I even forgave God for what I perceived as the needless suffering He allowed to go on in the world.

In this moment of breakthrough, I came to understand that the judgments I held about others were the very same obstacles that separated me from my personal relationship with God. Since then, this flowing sense of forgiveness has never left.

One year later, in the summer of 2008, I was asked to come to Hawaii for a few weeks to help draft a manual for spiritual leadership. I was to be assisted by two other disciples, both of whom were being intensely worked with by Kalindi.

From the moment I arrived, Kalindi ignored me, spending all her time working with the other disciples. I was left to work on the manual on my own. Time passed. Two weeks extended to six weeks, and still I didn't know when I would go home. I felt rejected and that pissed me off. I flashed back to childhood feelings of abandonment. I was separated from both my spiritual master and my daughter who eagerly awaited my return.

These feelings overflowed into action when our stay got extended yet again. I told my fellow disciples that I'd hit my limit and was leaving, but first I had to see Kalindi to say goodbye. By the time I met with Kalindi, I was crying hysterically. I knelt at her feet and held onto her ankles, saying, "I'm sorry but I can't do this anymore. I can't leave Kaya for months on end when I told her I'd be gone for no more than a few weeks. And I can't stand feeling shut out by you when you are so physically near."

Having made these admissions, I thought Kalindi would kick me out of the Mission. Instead, she did what I least expected. She guided me into a connection with God unlike any other I have ever known.

First, she allowed me to sob out my sorrow while lying at her feet. Then, she put her hand on the base of my spine and pressed hard. Slowly, Kalindi moved her hand up the spinal cord to my neck. As she did this, she spoke to me about my childhood. She said it was safe now to let the fear come fully to the surface. She promised that nothing bad would happen. She said I could handle it. And as I let go of the fear, she encouraged me to let the energy move through my body. She told me to let it build up toward the top of my head. All the while, she kept her hand moving on my back. Once the energy reached my throat chakra, Kalindi instructed me to scream as hard as I could into a towel. She said this would shoot the previously blocked energy out the top of my head. Through this opening, she took me deeper and deeper into the most powerful connection with Gourasana's energy that I'd ever had.

As the fear literally poured out of my body through the crown chakra,[1] the energy of the Lord poured in. In this state, Kalindi had me get up off the floor and dance with her. I danced into an ecstatic connection. Wave after wave of His presence poured into me as I moved deeper and deeper into my true self in God. Gourasana calls this a 'true-self connection.' At last, I'd let go completely. Finally I carried something of the presence of the Lord within me. Little did I know that this was just the beginning of my personal relationship with Him.

---

[1] The crown chakra is the energy center in the body located at the top of the head, directly in the middle. It is generally considered to be the chakra of 'pure consciousness,' symbolized by the lotus flower.

CHAPTER 10

GETTING THE NEWS

I never thought I would write a book about my spiritual transformation, nor did I think I would get diagnosed with a malignant brain tumor at the age of fifty-one. Then again, it is only because of the tumor that I now awaken daily to the depth of my connection to God. Just as daily what is unnecessary falls away.

Lately, even my sense of priorities has shifted. Only a while ago my 'terminal' story was about holding on to whatever I could of the physical, emotional, and personal me. I wanted longevity and vitality. I wanted continued association with my peers. I wanted to continue being a mother. There was a sense of unfinished business that burned in me. Now, the affairs and concerns of life are nowhere near as intriguing or inviting.

This transition began several years before I knew I had cancer. The symptoms of illness first showed up in the way I interacted with others. Inexplicably my behavior began to change. I morphed from this competent, energetic, intelligent adult into someone subject to waves of anxiety and odd compulsions. I went from being steady and reliable to someone constantly knocked off her stride.

I started seeking help from psychiatrists and using psychotropic drugs to alleviate the worst of the apprehension and compulsiveness. Nothing brought me back to balance. Nothing stopped the downward spiral. I became more and more forgetful and out of touch with reality until just being around me became unnerving for everyone, including me.

By the end of 2009, I was subject to mild seizures. Even so, it was not until May 2010 that a housemate who is also a nurse witnessed one of my seizures as we sat together in our living room. She insisted that I see a neurologist immediately. Within a week, I had an MRI and soon thereafter, a biopsy. Within no time I was back in the doctor's office to receive 'the news.'

I was told that I had an aggressive form of cancer in both frontal lobes of the brain known as an oligodendroglioma. It was too large and too close to my speech center to be surgically removed. I was told that the tumor might have been growing in my brain for up to ten years. It was the cause of my odd behavior and soon might affect my speech and other brain functions. It was Grade Three (out of Four), malignant and invasive. If not dealt with aggressively, the cancer could kill me within a short period of time.

My first reaction was shocked disbelief. Right after receiving this terrible news, I went to lunch with J.M. and several other close friends. My stomach was in my throat. I was speechless and couldn't even cry. I just kept hearing the words "huge" and "Stage Three" echoing in my ears.

As soon as the food was ordered, I started to apologize for my behavior. In the middle of this apology, one of my friends (who is also a doctor) warned me not to identify with this monster of guilt that had me judging myself about how I had behaved when there was no choice in the matter. He recommended I find acceptance and said no one was to blame. Yes,

Chapter 10

I had a horrible disease; yes, it was natural to be overwhelmed by dread; and yes, it was also treatable even if it was not curable.

It took days for the initial panic to wear off. Once it did, I got to work. I was determined to make my life and environment conducive to spiritual consciousness and healing. This meant taking care of business, everything completed and in its place, nothing unfinished and nothing blocking my connection with God.

The surgeon who did my biopsy introduced me to a well known oncologist, Dr. Ed Arenson, the head of the Hematology/Oncology Department at the Swedish Medical Center in Englewood, Colorado. As I quickly learned, once I was in his care, Dr. Arenson is a man of great compassion, a wise man, a holy man. He is also an artist. The walls of his office are filled with his colorful, free-flowing art.

Swedish Medical Center offers support groups for Dr. Arenson's patients, followed by healing services that Dr. A leads himself. The services include live musicians, poetry readings and an altar representing many religions. That his altar is so like Kalindi's altar in its embrace of all world religions made me feel so welcome and comfortable in the good doctor's presence.

At the core of Dr. A's practice lies a passionate belief that God's hand is involved in everything Dr. A does, from painting to the love and care of those afflicted with brain and spinal tumors. In my case, Dr. A proposed a very aggressive treatment program.

When I first entered Dr. A's care, I was less engaged in preparing for the end and more optimistic that chemotherapy and radiation would destroy the tumor and I would go on about my life. I should have known better. As they say, the writing was on the wall. From the beginning, I was warned that I would never return to my former state of normal brain function and thereby regain full mental acuity. No matter what, my intellectual capacity would continue to diminish, and who I thought I was before my diagnosis would never be me again.

Dr. A mapped out a year-long treatment program. All told, I had eight rounds of chemotherapy over a ten-month period. Because the chemo 'cocktail' I took caused my platelets to drop precipitately, I received seven platelet transfusions all told and, ultimately, had to end the program early.

I felt such a letdown when forced to stop this course of treatment. I wanted the chemotherapy to do its job and then to be done with it. After ten months, my sense of optimism took a blow. Even so, my MRIs suggested that the treatment had been relatively successful. It had done what it was supposed to do; the tumor had shrunk considerably.

Now I had to build my immune system back before beginning radiation. It took six weeks before Dr. A gave me the go-ahead. For the next seven weeks I received radiation every day five days a week. I was told that radiation would be a piece of cake compared to chemotherapy. I found it harder. I was tired most of the time and had frequent headaches. Then I began to isolate myself when my hair started falling out.

**Getting my head shaved by Gina,
my caregiver, in June 2011**

Chapter 10   KAREN TENNEY

Bald and beautiful

Both chemo and radiation made me feel sick. I was queasy practically all the time. Smoking marijuana was the only thing that helped to settle the waves of nausea. I tried to smoke only when necessary, and eventually caught on to using a vaporizer instead of a pipe to spare my lungs. Although the chemo was physically challenging, it was not until I started radiation that I began to lose my hair. It came out in clumps, leaving bald spots here and there. I couldn't stand to watch it. So, like many cancer patients before me, I shaved my head.

During this time the nausea caused by radiation wasn't the only thing that churned me up inside. On one level, losing my hair was small potatoes. Even the thought of death was not so terrible when set beside loss of brain function. To lose my mind was utterly appalling.

My first reaction after hearing what might happen to my mind was to think, "Oh, shit! I'm going to be a mentally-challenged person who eventually turns into a vegetable." How can I break free without that mental sharpness Kalindi refers to on so many of her talks? Isn't mental acuity a prerequisite for breaking the cycle of birth and death? And yes, beneath it all skulked this belief that a big part of my self-worth was tied up in my superior intelligence.

Brainpower was one of my greatest attributes. I was born bright. "Be sharp!" "Wake up!" Kalindi would often say to us. What was my fate if I became dull-witted?

These fears washed over me completely after Kalindi died. When I turned to The Lady to ask if losing my mind would destroy all chance of making it Home, she assured me that one's spiritual awareness operates outside the confines of the mind. On a phone call in December 2010, she told me that a brain tumor may affect my ability to function in the material world, but it wouldn't impair my connection to God. Her exact words were:

> *If your consciousness is fully immersed in Home and desire, even while this [brain tumor] goes on in the material body, you have your connection. That's what you're striving for.*

Even as I was afraid for my mind, I was also aware that somehow I was less afraid in general. I can't say when this began. I do know that it began soon after the diagnosis, and it came as a completely unexpected blessing. None of the diagnoses or treatments frightened me, not even when I needed platelet transfusions to bolster my depleted bone marrow. For me this response was very strange. Fear had been such a close companion throughout my life. Where once I'd regularly chanted Kalindi's warning, "Don't let the fear stop you," now I realized there is practically nothing left for me to fear.

It feels like the presence of God now fills those spaces once controlled by fear. As an added benefit, there is much less struggle around what I must give up. For example, during my cancer treatment, I gave up driving because of the potential side effects. I was subject to seizures and bouts of exhaustion. At the same time, I gave up virtually all social interaction because of my depleted immune system. During those days

I felt particularly unwell, I gave up spending time with my daughter. Even though I had found a feeling of peace about dying, I was still determined to give it my best shot to beat this thing. Why else would I fly to Brazil to see John of God thirty-six hours after my last radiation treatment?

John of God and Giving Up Hope

John of God, February 2012

João de Deus or John of God has a worldwide reputation as one of the most powerful mediums alive. He may well be the most famous healer presently on earth. João is a humble man with no formal medical training. According to him, he gives over his consciousness to the spirits of former doctors and known saints. These entities present teachings, give talks, and examine the thousands who line up to receive their counsel. When called for, the entities conduct visible and invisible (i.e., energetic rather than hands-on) operations that are scheduled three days a week at the Casa. Since João discovered his gift as a teenager more than half a century ago, some fifteen million people have been treated at the Casa. John claims on his website:

> *I do not cure anybody. God heals, and in His infinite goodness permits the Entities to heal and console my brothers. I am merely an instrument in God's divine hands.*

On the second day of my trip, The Lady called me, not knowing that I had flown to Brazil. Her reaction and guidance were clear. On our phone call of August 2, 2011, she said:

> *If you are going [to see John of God] searching for miraculous healing, you are making a spiritual mistake. Ultimately you have to give up hope. . . . This state is paramount to achieving a high state of God consciousness before death. Everything must be given up, except your hope in God. God must become your only solace. . . . This is a serious juncture for you.*

In my response to The Lady, I said I would meditate on her guidance, and that I wasn't sure if I should have come to Brazil at all. I even wavered about what to do that afternoon when I was scheduled to have a 'spiritual surgery' (energetic, rather than physical). Having already come to Brazil with a friend who would have had to leave with me, I chose to stay and keep the appointment. It was a very difficult decision for me, but in a way I had no choice. I didn't have the strength at that point to fly back to the U.S., especially not on my own.

After the procedure I went into a twenty-four-hour recovery period during which there were to be no distractions. During that post-operative period, I was brought my meals in bed and otherwise instructed to do nothing but sleep, pray, and meditate. My prayer was:

Father, please purify me of all illusion before I stand before you at the time of my death.

I prayed that prayer continuously. Even during the sixteen hours that I slept the prayer stayed with me. During sleep I also revisited scenes from my life. It felt as though I made a return trip to Varanasi, India, a holy place of pilgrimage for Hindus who come to purify themselves in the sacred waters of the Ganges. Everything goes on in that river: laundry is washed, children are bathed, people die and are cremated, and in my dream, I bathed as one of the multitude who came for healing and purification.

Later, I floated in and out of my childhood. The scenes came and went. In one of them, I was sledding in Central Park with my older brother. In another, I was splashing water over my baby brother's body, bathing him as I had bathed myself in the Ganges.

I even saw myself in that bed in my hotel room in Brazil. Only now, instead of a clean and airy compartment, all around me was piss and shit on the floor. If I got off the bed, I would have to step in it. The stench was horrible. I thought I would suffocate. And then it was over, and I was being picked up by the 'Light Beings' who came *en masse* to gather me up in their company. Somehow, I knew that each of those dreams was directly related to my purification.

When I awoke, I thought about what The Lady had said, that "God must become my only solace." There were no more treatments for me to follow. Neither the conventional nor the unconventional could keep me alive. Everything I'd been doing with an eye to recovery was driven by my desire to live. And now, at the end of that twenty-four hours, I had come to a much different perspective.

For me to achieve ultimate freedom, I must change my consciousness. The way I'd held myself inside was no longer appropriate. It was this The Lady was addressing. I wrote The Lady the following response:

> *Friday, August 5, 2011*
> *Dearest Lady,*
> *The guidance you gave me when we spoke a few days ago made me look long and hard at the gravity of my predicament once again. I have been asking myself some questions I hadn't asked before:*
>
> - *Did I come to Brazil to see John of God for miraculous healing?*
> - *Do I maintain hope that healing from the cancer at this stage is even possible?*
> - *Am I approaching my life and my treatment from the highest God consciousness I possibly can?*
>
> *After we spoke, I spent the next twenty-four hours in prayer and meditation, seeking answers. Even though I do not believe I will ever be completely free from this cancer, I understand now that I will not advance as fast as I need to spiritually to break free in this lifetime if I continue to allow the mechanism of denial and false hope to go on.*
>
> *The truth is that I have sought to prolong my life through whatever healing modalities I have chosen over the past year, which is not wrong in and of itself, but the serious mistake I have made is to not pursue the highest consciousness you are directing me toward: that is, to put all of my hope in God and have Him be "my only solace." This seems to be the main teaching I return to again and again: Find comfort in Him and Him alone.*

Chapter 10

The Lady offered me so much help from the beginning of this journey. She implored me not to waste time looking for a miraculous cure, but to focus instead on my desire for the Lord. Because of her guidance, I came to understand how much time I have wasted hanging on to false hopes based on my expectations of how life should be. I also realized how often I open the door to negative thoughts, judgments and discouragement. None of these belongs in the repertoire of someone dying. Kalindi says that at the time of death, "The only thing that matters is the love of God." The Lady suggested that, in my current state, now would be a good time to let go of everything but my desire for Home.

As always, my daughter, Kaya, stood by me even when she did not understand where I was going and what I must do to get there. Kaya and I have a history of facing things together. Two years ago, it was a breast cancer scare. One year later, I had cysts in my uterus that precipitated a hysterectomy. Then came the wrongly diagnosed anxiety/depression as being psychologically based. At the end, when it was discovered that I had Stage Three brain cancer, Kaya was there, yet again my bravest advocate. This snapshot of my illnesses added up to a lot of demands on a child who had not yet turned twelve.

Kaya has experienced more than her fair share of grief. She knows that even the boundless depth of my love for her cannot create a large enough crucible to hold all of her feelings about my dying and her having to carry on without me. She and I both know that in all likelihood, I will not be here as she grows into womanhood. At first, this disturbed her deeply and broke my heart. Now it is this fact of life that we both accept. Kaya also knows that even in my mothering of her, God takes precedence.

Sometimes her feelings boil over into anger and she turns on me. When things get really bad, she likes to bait me into fighting, and then gets angrier still because I have neither the energy nor the desire to fight. She wants me to fight with her – and for life – and I just don't feel drawn to fighting about anything anymore.

Everyone's experience when facing illness is uniquely personal. There is little about my path that can be described as universal. Each of us is as unique in our dying as we are in living. For some, terminal illness is a sacred time; for others it is dreaded and bleak. In facing death, I have had to confront the fact that I have been asleep for who knows how many lifetimes, and now I have the chance to wake up. It's time to recognize that God is the only reality. There is nothing but God, and my longing for God is the one desire I can count on as pure.

One morning recently, I woke up from a sound sleep, turned on my recorder, and said, "I hate this disease. I want out of this body." I begged Him, "Please Lord, give me the courage to face whatever I must. Please put Your arms around me. Please help me to know and follow Your will, not mine."

In October 2011, The Lady told me:

> *You can help people by how you go through this. This period is even more important than your birth. You are contributing to conscious departure.*

A good friend who also faces terminal illness wrote to me recently to share about her own suffering. She wrote,

> *Suffering is a paradox for someone searching for God. On a spiritual level, it is a benediction that drives you deeper into a serious, quiet and disciplined lifestyle otherwise not found so easily.*

The paradox came into play, she went on to say, when emotional and physical suffering deplete the body, and sometimes we have no choice but to bend to the limitations brought on by illness. Sometimes there is nothing to do but rest. It is while resting that we can choose to go deeper into a conscious connection to God or disappear into the suffering in the body. Bottom line, what is required is practice. Illness allows such a practice to blossom. In this practice, the suffering becomes a gift that allows God to take over body, mind, heart and soul. Rather than wonder why I am ill or combating how it feels, I now experience the gift that illness brings as I become less involved in all that I once believed was real.

Did I even know such desire before the cancer? I don't think so, not even when I felt trapped with nowhere to turn. I have come to believe that this tumor is my great liberator. It is like my 'Bodhi Tree.'[1] The cancer allows me to see that it is possible for me to achieve ultimate freedom in this lifetime, just as it is possible that I might not.

In our phone conversation on January 1, 2011, The Lady told me that everyone has to be so open-minded at the time of death. They cannot assume anything. She said,

> *You have to be so open-minded. . . . Even [though] you might take birth again . . . your meditation should be about not taking birth again. We all may take birth again, but the emphasis . . . for you, because you have strong desire to break the cycle of birth and death, [comes in] turning to Him and bringing Him to you.*

It still shocks me when The Lady includes herself as someone who must never stop endeavoring to break free. This, in spite of the fact that Kalindi told us that The Lady is already free. It makes me recognize that there are no limits to the humility one must have with God because God *is* Humility. The Lady carries that kind of humility. It seems to be the most natural, innate part of her being. It has not been like that for me. I have to pray every day of my life for humility. It is not so easily attainable.

---

[1] The Bodhi Tree is a large, very old sacred fig tree under which Siddhartha achieved enlightenment, or 'Bodhi,' after which he became known as Gautama Buddha.

Kalindi also said that everything we do toward breaking free becomes part of our 'spiritual bank account' that only increases in value. From life to life, it is always there for the soul to draw upon. This gives me some reassurance that every effort I make counts, even if I think it doesn't matter if I do not break free this time around.

For the first fifty years of my life, I was like most people, frittering away time in distracting pursuits. I was all about, "Eat, drink and be merry . . ." I had not thought about, ". . . for tomorrow we may die." Even after I was diagnosed with cancer, I hung onto my distractions. The ultimate example of this took place in November 2010. While receiving chemotherapy, I went on Match.com in search of male companionship. At the same time, I went on several skiing excursions, priding myself on being able to engage in challenging physical activities just like I'd done when I was healthy.

When The Lady heard about these pursuits, she suggested a course correction. She gave me guidance to stop both on-line dating and engaging in other 'material pastimes.' She made me realize I was choosing playthings over God. As this realization sank in, I wrote to The Lady saying I would:

- *Disengage from material pleasures that bind me to the flesh*
- *Turn my back on the world by entering into a quieter, deeper and more purposeful lifestyle*
- *Seek forgiveness in my heart from people in my life that I've transgressed and offended*
- *Reach out to and associate with people in the Mission in a loving way*
- *Work diligently on this monograph as promised*

Once doors like these began to open, I realized that I was now facing the 'Grand Illusion.' In one of her teachings, Kalindi talks about the Grand Illusion as being this shared conviction that everyone believes: I am not going to die.

Because even the longest life is over in a flash, Kalindi warns us that neither past nor future has value. Only the here and now matters. Even so, the Grand Illusion seduces us with memories from the past and hopes for the future while creating the feeling that somehow we can rewrite the former, control the latter and, as an encore, live each day as though we have forever.

I venture that this is how 99.9 percent of the people on earth treat death. It may happen to others, just not to me, just not today and not right now. Kalindi guides us to wake up to the fact that death comes for everyone. It comes when we are ready and when we are not.

According to Kalindi, next in line behind the Grand Illusion is 'illusory love.' The world over, people of every culture and nationality try to find completion outside the self. We seek for it with another person. We believe it can be found at work or through some belief system. We look to attain fulfillment in moment-to-moment experience that never completes us. Unlike the love of God, this form of love is temporary. It is filled with expectation. We believe it will go on forever, but it never does. One or the other person changes or dies. The business closes. The belief system breaks down. We pass through a dark night of the soul and all bets are off. At the end, we realize that nothing of this earth can last. Only God is eternal, and to the eternal we must turn if we are to end the cycle of reincarnation.

My illness brought this teaching into focus; with it came a greater seriousness that made me both more conscious and conscientious. Even when all I wanted was to escape, I had no choice but to face my death. Until I did, the feelings of dread would only get worse.

My relationship to physical suffering has also dramatically changed. From early childhood I have a history of avoiding suffering. After the cancer diagnosis, I had to make a choice to either go into greater denial or face the suffering head on. I chose the latter. Now when my physical symptoms are at their worst and the pain threatens to consume me,

God brings me to stillness and silence. In this place, I can best hear His whispers. This listening helps to fuel my faith and deepen my trust. In this state, I feel worthy of His Love and grateful that my soul's purpose is fulfilled. At these times, there is no guilt or shame and no room for ego. Truly, there is grace in a suffering that brings with it fulfillment.

Chapter 11

The Come into the Light Ashram (2011)

The fruit of silence is prayer.

The fruit of prayer is faith.

The fruit of faith is love.

The fruit of love is service.

The fruit of service is peace.

Mother Teresa

In 2009, Kalindi created the Come into the Light Ashram for her most advanced disciples. In speaking about the purpose of the Ashram to Lara Lyndy,[1] Kalindi said,

---

[1] Lara Lyndy is an upcoming 'Break-Free' master named by Kalindi as carrying special energy from Gourasana to help those who desire it to break the cycle of birth and death. Lara leads the Come into the Light Ashram on several continents.

> *People are breaking free of binding illusions . . . so they can move forward with God. [When] letting go of the illusion . . . [there are] tools . . . to stay in the light and not get captured by illusion any more.*
>
> Kalindi, January 20, 2009

The Ashram in which I participated took place in September 2011. It was meant for 'reviewers,' meaning those who had participated in such an Ashram before. I was one of two newbies, both of us facing life-threatening illnesses and both of us very honored to participate. This marked the first time that anyone with serious health issues had entered this Ashram. I was recuperating from my cancer treatments and planned to be in the Ashram for one week out of the three scheduled. The day after the Ashram began I had to leave because I caught a cold. Three days later, I went back in and stayed until the Ashram ended.

The moment I entered the Come into the Light Ashram, I was asked to be in silence. At first, I had difficulty remaining silent and had to be reminded that this was my guidance. Silence has been part of my guidance off and on for years. Kalindi first introduced me to silence over a two-month period in Hawaii in 1999 when she directed me to stay silent when in her presence. She knew silence would directly confront my ego and told me that when I was silent more of my true self would come through.

For me being silent required tremendous focus and effort. I had such an urge to speak at times that I could not hold my tongue. Kalindi would jab me in the side when I offered a suggestion, saying, "Better not to speak." I would swallow my words and fall back mutely, stunned by the audacity of my own ego which, even when hushed, continued on inside my head insisting that what I had to say had value.

Over the years, as silence became part of my spiritual discipline, it took me into a deeper relationship with God. Through silence Kalindi taught me the importance of thinking before speaking, and thereby how to control what comes out of my mouth.

In the Come into the Light Ashram, I discovered a big secret. At least it was big to me. I learned that turning toward the light is always and only *a decision*. Deciding to stay in the light requires discerning truth from illusion. Each time illusion is identified, I *decide* to confront it or turn away. It can control me or I can deny it. Sometimes it is a form of control to dissect how the illusion works with me. Sometimes, entering God's flow of energy is all I am called to do. Whether I shine light on it or turn away from it, the illusion shrivels in the brilliance of God's light.

Even as my practice grows stronger, the illusion can still make a mess of things. I'd been in the Come into the Light Ashram for only a few days when the participants were asked by Lara to go out together for dessert. I declined, replying, "No, thank you. I would only be doing it to be social." As a result, powerful spiritual help and guidance came to me personally as the group prepared to leave. Through an intermediary, Lara asked, "What you do you think this is, a pick-and-choose game?" Her words stung. They made me ask myself, "Am I here to exercise my preferences or to follow the direction for the group? Where is my willing surrender?"

Right then, I saw how I separated myself from others, not only in the Ashram but also in my life in general. I felt entitled to choose to go or stay based on my own preferences and concepts of what was best for me. I was not at one with my fellow participants or the Ashram's consciousness. Regardless of my health issues, going out for dessert became important. It provided the perfect opportunity to practice giving up separate will. Humbled by this recognition, I joined my Ashram mates, and the separation disappeared.

I was even more aware of the difference the very next morning when I awoke feeling light of heart. Later I joined my Ashram mates in meditation. As a massive surge of energy filled the room, some version of an awakening, or illumination, happened for me and others. Suddenly there was a palpable oneness among us, a connection that stayed with me throughout the Ashram.

In that deep dive into the light, a kind of clarity came to the surface. Things began to add up. Because of the illness, I'd been spending much of my time alone and in silence. Silence was already a major part of my daily life. The silence I experienced in the Ashram allowed me to go deeper, stay calmer and become more connected. It called forth a truer part that reflects more of what lives in my soul. The more I sought silence, the more I could quiet the mind and its chatter.

I came to see how spoken words and mental gymnastics were essential to my 'social personality' or character. The less I focused on this (little) self, the more light poured in, the sweeter the connection, the louder the whispers of God. The more I listened to the whispers, the less I needed to understand what was going on.

Forward movement requires a desire for change. And change was what Kalindi said God was all about. She told us repeatedly, "Change, change, change and keep changing. Change something every day." A willingness to change means there is less time to linger over what is frightening. Gourasana warned in His *Sign Book*, "Don't let the fear stop you" (p. 6). Kalindi promised that when we confront and go through fear, like any other emotion, we see it for what it is – the illusion's last-ditch effort to slow us down or have us give up the effort altogether.

Calling on the Name "Gourasana"

At my very first Intensive, Kalindi encouraged us to call on the name Gourasana to invoke the personal presence of God. From the moment I first saw Him in the flesh in 1994, Gourasana made Himself known to me. When I looked into His eyes, I saw reflected back love coupled with lifetimes of desire to know God as real. I loved Gourasana instantly. He became the One closest to my heart from the moment we met. He has been there ever since. All along the way, He has brought a rich, real and unique love into my life. Since my illness, He has become my protection and comfort. The love I feel for Gourasana, Kalindi and The Lady is the most special love I have ever known. Truly, I love each of them more than life itself.

It is not necessary for others to call on Gourasana's name to feel His loving presence. He does not require belief in order to access His assistance. The energy of God does not need to be named in order to be experienced. But for me, to call on Gourasana or sing His name is to become immersed in my personal connection with the Father (i.e., the energy and presence of God, the Father of all creation).

The more I trust Gourasana's powerful energy, the easier it is for me to surrender to the will of God. Finally, after years on this Path, I realize that the will of God is my soul's true will. Only in duality can God and I be separate. And only by free will can this separation end.

Accepting His will allows me to 'listen, say yes and act,' whether or not I like or even understand His message. Listen, say yes and act[2] is an essential teaching from Gourasana. The essence of this teaching is that true hearing requires action. 'Right action' is discovered through meditation where one accesses 'higher intelligence' vs. making decisions from the mind, with all its fears, concepts and limitations. As distinct from the mind, higher intelligence comes from our connection to God and His will for us.

Finding this depth of listening and action became critical during my illness, especially during and after chemo and radiation when the symptoms of illness overwhelmed me. There was no rhythm to my life. I had to change everything; my body gave me no choice. Even how I

---

[2] I first saw this teaching as a sign on the wall at my first Intensive. It is foundational to understanding how to travel the Path quickly and with as little resistance as possible.

meditated changed. Physically, I had to lie down rather than get up. Spiritually, I had to stop begging God to come and start knowing God was here. In all ways, I had to take on a much more disciplined lifestyle. Having a disciplined lifestyle is part of the practice Kalindi spent years teaching us.

This disciplined lifestyle of rapid transformation (also termed 'The Lifestyle') became the very first Spiritual Advancement Course (SAC) offered in 1999 by Miracle of Love. In it, we were taught how to live in the material world in God consciousness as well as how to remove unnecessary distractions from our spiritual pursuit.

'The Lifestyle' includes how to (1) communicate to others clearly and respectfully; (2) organize our belongings and files; (3) pack our bags with necessities in case of an emergency; (4) use a system that prioritizes the next most important thing to do as a means of clearing our minds and allowing needed information to come in; and (5) get enough exercise, rest and sleep to best function in the world while transforming spiritually at a rapid speed. It is largely because of The Lifestyle that I found patience, calm and love for myself during my illness.

In the Ashram, I began to experience days filled with serious and sober urgency. The inner landscape became more real and fulfilling. Still, it wasn't all light and roses. There was a period of time when I felt beckoned by the devil – the 'darkness,' 'Lucifer,' 'Maya Devi' – whatever one calls the evil that lurks inside and out and poisons our hearts. This darkness showed up in the form of self-doubt. "Can I trust what is happening? Can I keep up with the others? Am I worthy of God's Love?"

When the darkness crept in, I called on Gourasana to lift me back into the Light. And He did. It was almost like flipping a switch. I also listened to His talk "The Beautiful Gem" (1994) over and over again. At times, I would read the transcript as I listened to His voice. There is something so powerful about seeing His words as He speaks them. In "The Beautiful Gem," He addresses the pervasive illusion of unworthiness:

> *This is a universal problem that everybody has to some degree or another. . . . And that is a lack of self-worth. . . . A lot of people won't even approach God. And the primary reason that they won't make a serious endeavor to get God in this lifetime is because they don't feel that they are worthy. They don't feel that God is going to accept them because they are so bad, because they are so unworthy. But of course this is only the illusion covering everybody over. . . .*
>
> *God never sees the illusion . . . the illusion isn't who you are. . . . No matter how bad you are, God never ever sees you in any other way than [as] a pure Being of Light and a precious gem in this material world.*

There was a period in the Ashram when I wanted to be filled with more light. I danced by myself in the closet to songs that I love and can move to. I have always found that music feeds my connection and opens me up to feel more love. Like so many of my generation, I found this connection to music as a teenager. I would sit in my room for hours and listen to songs that empowered me and songs that made me cry. I couldn't explain it but I knew my feelings were real.

Snow Patrol's "Just Say Yes" became my Ashram's theme song. "Yes" to pulling in more of His energy, light and love for everyone. "Yes" to giving more of myself to Him every day. "Yes" to coming Home to Him as fast as possible. "Yes, yes, yes" to whatever He asks of me.

Sometimes, my body succumbed to the side effects of the cancer treatments. There were days when I slept for hours. When I awoke, I sometimes felt disappointed that my body couldn't perform like everybody else's. I grew restless, even when exhausted. In this weakened condition, I kept thinking I had somewhere to go, something to do, some schedule to keep. This went on for days until finally, exhaustion itself forced me to change. The moment I did, what had been a burden became an opportunity to live more fully in God's timing. No matter how I felt, the day-to-day belonged to Him. In this change, I learned how to practice self-love and once again sought out silence and deep meditation. With meditation came the message that, as I conserved my energy and went deeper, so I starved my ego. My mind grew still, and time passed during which a dense and weighty cloud that had covered me over lifted off and dissipated.

Throughout the Ashram I went through a series of self-examinations. In the silence of my room and my personal connection with God, I exposed my shortcomings and renewed my respect for what it takes to resist the illusion.

Gourasana says in Quote #384,

> *Every type of suffering is waiting for those who choose to stay on this plane of existence. Still they decide to stay. This is because of the incredible power of the illusion.*
>
> *Breaking the Cycle of Birth and Death* (p. 119)

Gourasana also tells us that all limitation is illusory, just as there is no limit to the ecstasy and love we can feel right now. Heaven does not come afterwards. The soul does not need the body to die in order to become free. The soul breaks free while housed in a body. It takes trust and faith to make it Home – and one single condition – that we 'never give up.'[3]

On many talks and in several books, Kalindi schools us in the core teaching to 'never give up.' She tells us that no one knows what God has in store for us or anyone else. She reminds us to always strive to come

---

[3] The Lady spoke in the July 2000 Intensive about David Swanson's "Rules to Live By" and about his extraordinary qualities. She said that to 'never give up' was the one quality David claimed to have, and it was that one quality that allowed him to make it Home when he and Gourasana departed in 1995.

closer to God and give more of ourselves to Him every day. She teaches that sometimes the hardest thing to do is to accept God's mysterious ways. It takes so much trust and faith when we face that mystery.

In all of her guidance, Kalindi never steered me wrong. She always brought me closer to God. Because of her I learned acceptance, even when I did not understand. Kalindi used to laugh about her 'bad hair days.' She used to say that material life is not easy, even after we fully accept God into our lives. We live in the 'land of illusion,' a place of suffering that is hard on the body and soul, no matter which hand of cards we are dealt.

One day, I got an internal message, "Don't ask. Just go. Give yourself to Him. Whatever transpires, go through it. Be willing to make mistakes and be a fool for God." It was like I was being told to be on the lookout for opportunities to take chances and think outside my spiritual box. In no time, I got the chance to try. It happened on the day I celebrated my birthday. It was a difficult day for me. I was filled with self-judgment, whereas just the day before, I felt the exact opposite. I went from gratitude for all I was accomplishing to believing I wasn't getting anywhere at all. I was utterly disturbed. And then I remembered my inner direction: "Don't ask. Just go. Give yourself to Him."

Further help came when I remembered Kalindi's guidance about 'the three most obvious signs of the illusion':

> *As the light increases, the illusion tries to bother you with the three most obvious signs. Don't fall prey to negative thoughts, judgments, or discouragement. Do not allow it. Meditate. Scream. Dance. Talk to a friend. Write every day to your [spiritual] leader.*
>
> *Remember, I am holding you.*
>
> Kalindi, February 17, 2008

On the subject of the three most obvious signs, Kalindi spoke to me personally when I was with her in Hawaii in 2008. She said,

> *If you feel any of these, meditate immediately; then sit and figure it out. Don't buy into it. Just sit down and figure out why you are negative and then write down on paper what you are going to do to move it. It is a complete phantom and has to be dissolved.*

This guidance came back to me that day. There I was, lying flat on my back hounded by self-judgment. It was time to meditate, but I was too tired to move. I played sweet songs, wild songs, any songs. I cried and cried. I cried when I got up to dance, and I cried when the fatigue dumped me back into bed. I just wanted to die, right then and there. This was not about my suffering body. I'd just had enough and didn't want anymore. I felt done with material existence. There was nothing to live for, no matter my responsibilities as a mother or as someone who had promised to write this book. I was worn down to nothing and overwhelmed by the weight of life.

Then, instead of fatigue, I was overcome by urgency. I felt driven into His arms while simultaneously scooped up out of my suffering. I only wanted to go where God was taking me. I only wished to be filled by Him. Fulfillment and the end of suffering now came through willing surrender. Suddenly, the exhaustion no longer mattered. For the next several days I spent a great deal of time writing in my journal. I include some excerpts from that time:

September 29, 2011

> *Today, the Ashram's participants were told we are at a critical juncture. We've reached a stage of spiritual evolution in which we are connected, cared for, and shielded from the horrors of*

> *this world. In this state, the question becomes, "Where do we go from here?"*
>
> *We were told there is a limit to the being of illusion. We can choose to leap out of the false identity of ego and personality and into our true identity. It is as simple as leaving one room and stepping into another. It sounds so easy. But is it? Can it ever be?*
>
> *Then I realized it has already happened to me. I have broken through the separation again and again. I know what it feels like when the change comes. All anyone has to do is choose the Light over the darkness. Making the choice is the key! Holding onto that choice is the challenge.*

September 30, 2011

> *My breakthroughs come in unexpected ways. Yesterday, there was no fanfare. I simply saw with new eyes. Even when the energy amps up, I notice that I now move more easily into ecstasy and freedom rather than feeling out of control and confused. Just being in association in this Ashram pulls more of this energy to me.*

My journal entries have always been an important part of my spiritual practice as a chronicle of my transformation and a powerful tool guiding me onward. In the midst of these Ashram breakthroughs, I have learned to stop trying so hard to get to God. God already has me. I don't have to strive so hard to get there. That is all I need to know: "Be still and know that God is here."[4]

---

[4] Although spoken elsewhere, this quote was first spoken by Kalindi on a call she had with the Australian community in 2009. Later, it became a prayer.

Even when my mind realizes it is no longer captain of the ship, it still wants to be in control. Only when mastered and trained as an instrument of disciplined restraint can the mind be a useful tool. Otherwise, it is a jumble of self-serving conventions and preferences.

One night in the Ashram, I had another quiet breakthrough. I actually felt myself walk away from binding self-doubt. It just fell away. I entered my next 'spiritual room.' The transition was calm and delightful. The space felt natural and non-illusory. To get there took no effort. Once in my connection, the greater my desire, the more connected I felt. Even when hooked by illusion, I was able to pull in more light. Like a refrain, over and over again, I kept hearing Gourasana's quote from His *Sign Book,* (p. 60):

> *Give up who you think you are. You are not that being of illusion.*
>
> *Give up who you **think** you are. You are **not** that being of illusion.*
>
> *Give up who you think you are.* **You are not that being of illusion.**

As I draw in the light, I become more hip to how the illusion catches me off-guard and learn to respond faster with countermeasures. The more serious I become, the more devious the illusion is in trying to stop me. As has been the case since early childhood, my final frontier is often fear – fear of letting go of what I know as 'me' as well as fear of the unknown.

At the beginning of the Ashram, Lara sent me a note, encouraging me to "build a case of trust and faith" in God for what I am receiving. The more I trust, the swifter and easier the journey becomes. I discover that the light always prevails. Prayer fortifies the light. Prayer uplifts me even when I feel lost and afraid of what's to come. Prayer is the most powerful tool I know to dispel the darkness.

Since leaving the Ashram, I no longer feel the need to prove anything to anyone. I know I am worthy of God's Love. I feel myself illuminated by the light and power of Gourasana's energy. Best of all, I now stay in the light so much more of the time.

**Breaking into the Light in the Come into the Light Ashram,
September 2011**

CHAPTER 12

Conscious Departure

One question I have asked myself over and over again is how can I break the cycle of birth and death while I'm alive? How does anyone do that? How does a person let go of illusory consciousness and still inhabit duality? How does someone achieve full awareness when the world is made up of false hopes and dreams?

After years of watching Kalindi at work, I have come to know that it is possible to break free, just as I firmly believe that all of us will eventually achieve full union with God. Gourasana promised that every soul will eventually break free when they are truly ready to depart from material consciousness.

Without understanding how, I believe this is happening for me right now. In *Breaking the Cycle of Birth and Death* Gourasana tells us that "desire is everything,"[1] He adds that we are guaranteed success so long as

---

[1] In many of their talks, Gourasana and Kalindi teach that "desire is everything!" Gourasana says on His talk called "Desire" that it is the force that will move you from one place to another. Materially this principle is true, and spiritually it is essential. Also see Kalindi's talk, "Desire Is Everything."

we never give up. In referencing birth and death, Gourasana talks about the nature of existence.

In Quote #319, He says,

> *What is your existence all about? What is the point? There is only one thing for certain: that you exist to find the truth, to find the light, to find the love, to find the Lord, to return Home to the True Realm of Existence. Whatever else you may believe or feel, the conclusion that your existence here was never meant to be eternal is inescapable. Your existence is designed to culminate in your becoming aware. So become aware.*
>
> Gourasana, *Breaking the Cycle of Birth and Death* (p. 97)

First we must have an unyielding desire to leave this plane of illusion. Then we must find the spiritual fiber and faith to renew and even increase that desire as we face each attachment and give it up. In the end, before death, we must finish with every attachment. All desire for the things of this world must be complete.

This process is unique to each of us. It is neither passive nor vague. It is an *active* listening, an *active* search, and an *active* training to become ever more aware of what is truth and what is illusion.

In The Intensive, Kalindi taught us that we are bound to material existence by habits, concepts, beliefs and attachments that give us a false sense of the world as our home. Practically speaking, everyone is under the spell of the illusion. The express purpose of the illusion is to keep us bound to material consciousness. It takes *conscious choice* and serious endeavor to break the spell.

One of the great challenges we face concerns the body. We think the body matters. We think that what our minds conjure up is real. As we endeavor in day-to-day life and work to fix ourselves and others, not to mention the problems of this world, we believe that we are making spiritual advancement. The mind is so determined to hold sway that it refuses to believe that this material world is only temporary. The soul alone knows that our ultimate purpose is to find our way back to God. For that to happen, each person must wake up. Kalindi says,

> *This material existence is always, at best, in every single way, a world of false hopes and dreams. It always will be. You have left your true Home where everything exists eternally. . . . You have become so lost in this illusion, so lost, for so long, you can't even remember Home. So you keep trying to create a home in a false reality.*
>
> *The illusion has the specific job of keeping you lost and entangled in its web . . . for as long as possible until you cannot stand it any longer . . . and you know you want to return Home.*
>
> "World of False Hopes and Dreams"[2]

Kalindi teaches that God cannot pry us free if we do not wish to let go. We must come to God of our own free will. There is no place for 'separate will' in the spiritual journey. For me, it has taken guidance from Kalindi to distinguish between God's will and my will.

When I insist that there is something else to experience of the world, God satisfies that desire. God will not go against my separate will. I will incarnate again and again if that is my desire. We return to this plane of illusion until we are ready to fully unite with Him in the True Realm of Existence.[3] This union must take place while we are alive. We must find our way Home to God while still in a body. Over my two decades on this Path, I have glimpsed the true realm many times. I've even spent

---

[2] Kalindi, "World of False Hopes and Dreams," *The Bottom Line Series,* January 28, 1997.

[3] "The True Realm of Existence [is] also called 'Home.' It refers to the spiritual realm or spiritual plane of existence where the spirit soul resides with God." Kalindi, *The Break-Free Message*, (p. xix).

long stretches of time there. No matter what it is called in all world religions – from Heaven to Nirvana – it is my goal to be there eternally.

Departure from material existence can be conscious or not, but our *final* departure must be in full conscious awareness. When this happens, according to Buddhism, we get off the karmic wheel and achieve enlightenment. In Christianity we are judged by St. Peter, with only the few reckoned worthy to enter the Pearly Gates.

It was only after being diagnosed with cancer that I began to fully prepare to make such a passage. It took me months just to get my personal house in order. Part of this had to do with prioritizing my own desires. Was I caught up in matters of the world or those of God? And if of the world, why hang on to material concerns that I knew I'd have to give up eventually? Gourasana wrote to Maha (Kalindi's daughter) when she was only six years old, saying,

> *If you long for God, you will find God. The more you long for things of this world, the less likely it will be that you find God.*

There was such a split focus in my own life. Because the business of living had been so important to me, the business of dying became mesmerizing. Part of this business was necessary and part of it was not. Part of me longed for completion and part of me longed for the world. When my longing turned toward something or someone, a part of me was held back from God. Giving everything to God is not a one-time declaration. It is a step-by-step process. For so long as I live, there will always be further to go. The Lady taught me that by example.

I think of the many times I have clung to my daughter as a source of love in my life, even as I know that she is not the Source. The more I realize this, the more I let go of my attachment to her. The more I detach, the less guilt and sentimentality restrain me. Furthermore, my true relationship with Kaya now fully blossoms. The love between us is no longer clouded over with emotion and neediness.

Throughout history, it is rare to find people seeking union with the Divine living in the villages or cities of the world. Most of these seekers remove themselves, turning their backs on jobs and families. Kalindi wanted her disciples to live in the world. She said we would be 'yogis in the marketplace.' Unlike monks and saints of the past, our path is to carry on a normal existence while breaking free from that existence in our pursuit of God.

Today, there are thousands on this planet who have been touched by Kalindi, and perhaps millions more who share the belief that their soul has come to earth at this time for a specific reason. Few can articulate why, but all feel a part of some grand design, some greater destiny.

Even science now posits theories about alternative planes of existence. String Theory, often called The Theory of Everything, attempts to reconcile the known and unknown. It argues that though unobservable, extra dimensions must exist. The problem with theories is that they are filled with concepts and beliefs that come from the mind. I much prefer trust and faith based on my personal experiences of God.

To her disciples, Kalindi's life was defined by trust and faith from the moment she entered this world with Gourasana. As His first disciple, Kalindi became His 'Voice' and 'Spiritual Master for This World.' She opened herself fully to Goursana's energy in order to forge a path Home for others to follow. In this opening, she came to literally house His energy in the flesh.

The Lady came in with Gourasana and Kalindi. As Kalindi's first disciple, The Lady became the other living 'Spiritual Master for This World.' The Lady has a special destiny that keeps unfolding and expanding since Kalindi's passing.

The Lady's destiny was first given to her by Gourasana. On July 30, 1994, He said, "You and Kalindi are the leaders of this . . . all-important worldwide organization." Over the years Kalindi gave The Lady a Life

Plan. That plan includes a great number of tasks. Among these, The Lady is here to show the world how to pray, oversee those leading others in the use of the Modern-Day Meditation, work with the Mission's leaders as they bring Gourasana and Kalindi's teachings and programs to the world, and oversee key personnel in order to maintain spiritual purity.

Most important for me, The Lady has come to guide those seeking to go Home through 'conscious departure.' The offer to face my imminent departure consciously under The Lady's guidance came the moment she learned my diagnosis was terminal. She took me under her wing and gave me explicit guidance on how to prepare for death.

Uprooting the Ego

At first, The Lady concentrated on my ego or 'false self.' She warned me that the ego would work to stop me from achieving my ultimate goal. In order to lift off from material consciousness, the root of the ego needs to be completely exposed and destroyed. She reminded me of when Kalindi discussed 'the most insidious part of the ego.' Kalindi said the most insidious part of the ego is at the root of the ego's hold on this world. She called it the darkest force within us. In 2002, Kalindi offered a course known as The Strategy to Defeat the Illusion (aka 'The Strategy'). At the beginning of this course, she played a talk that describes the nature of this part of the ego:

> *For thousands of lifetimes, you have been building [the root of the ego]. It wants to continue to become greater. It actually wants to become God. [Because of it], even the most down-and-out person lying in the gutter secretly thinks he is greater than anyone else.*

Kalindi told us that the root of the ego feeds off the light of God and claims credit for any light brought in by God. This part of the ego touts itself as the source of light, giving no credit whatsoever to God.

If ultimate freedom is desired, the root of the ego must be exposed and what is holding it in place must be unraveled. It is the ego that loves to proclaim, "Look at me. I am God. I am the greatest being that ever lived."

After participating in several workshops designed to expose the root of the ego, I discovered that mine is grounded in wanting to be adored. Simultaneously, it expresses itself through self-abuse and self-hatred. Every time I see or feel that part of my ego, I pray to Gourasana to rip it out of me and destroy it. Sometimes I picture the Archangel Michael with his foot on the head of the demon, and I call upon him to defend me from its ubiquitous influence.

**Archangel Michael with his foot on Lucifer's head
(By Guido Reni)**

We were also given Gourasana's talk "How to Pray" (1995) to dispel the power of the most insidious part of the ego, the root of the ego. On this talk, Gourasana says,

> *It's just going to be one battle after another. You can win every battle that you are going to face. And it is important to have the trust and faith in Me to believe that this is true.*

In The Strategy, Kalindi also taught that the root of the ego attaches itself to each individual through a main ego trait. It is our job to find, expose and *stay* aware of how this trait controls every aspect of our being and personality.

According to Kalindi, there are four main ego traits: fear, self-righteousness, laziness and anger. If the ego is depicted as a tree (see illustration on the next page), the roots of the tree represent the root of the ego. The trunk is one's main ego trait, and the bigger branches are primary aspects of the ego. In my case, the root is my wanting to be adored. My trunk springs from fear, and the main branches are control, avoidance and feeling like a victim. The whole point of The Strategy is to uproot this tree in order to break free from the whole material predicament.

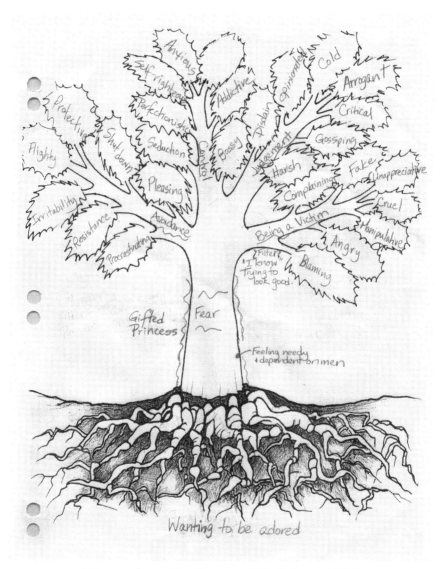

My tree from The Strategy Workshop, 2005

This tree represents how I have held myself in this body: how I walk, talk and present myself to the world. I can feel each one of these traits, especially control, as they manifest in my life and personality. I can feel them like fibrous threads running back through my life.

For example, it was my self-destructive fear of being hurt by others that drove me to bulimia. For seven years in my late 20's and early 30's, I was subject to eating my fill, leaving the table, running to the nearest bathroom and inducing vomiting. Then I would brush my teeth, wash my face and return to the table, hoping nobody noticed.

I inflicted this horrible form of punishment on myself through a distorted longing for love. I turned my yearnings for love into a sin for which bulimia was my punishment. I felt so abandoned by the people in my life. I wanted to be fulfilled. I thought this fulfillment came from another person. I had no idea that this was a love I could never find in the material world. Bulimia helped me to satiate an unbearable longing . . . at least for a little while. It hardly mattered that the enamel on my teeth was slowly eroding or that a knot of suppressed feelings coiled inside my intestines. It was only when my gum line started to noticeably recede, that I decided to seek help. Until then, no one – not my family or my friends – ever noticed what was going on with me.

I let my fear control almost everything, including the way I started and ended many of my relationships. I always did it on my timing and my terms. This is how I tried to protect my heart. The only problem was it never worked.

Now, after years on this path, I no longer speak of fear in an overarching way. Instead, I try to hone in on what specific fear I might be facing. Where today it is all about unraveling specific facets of fear, in the months following my cancer diagnosis in June 2010, feelings of entitlement and lack of worth continued to plague me. Somehow, I always had to have the last word. Those nearest me knew I was quick to defend myself. It didn't matter if I was being irrational; I was right. What a paradox. On the one hand, I was special and therefore deserving. On the other, I felt worthless.

I had no idea what it meant to be humble. For me, true humility was attached to shame and akin to unworthiness rather than a doorway to God. It took cancer and help from The Lady for humility to become real in my life.[4]

The Lady kindled in me the desire to find true humility before I died and the resolve to no longer distract myself in service to the ego. It took a lot to realize that 'having no distractions' does not mean rejecting bodily pleasures. I was not becoming a renunciate. I was not abandoning life; rather, I was coming to accept my death as part of my transformation back to Spirit.

The Lady's Guidance for Me on Conscious Departure

In October 2010, The Lady gave me the following information. She made it clear that it came from Kalindi and was meant to help prepare me for death. (*Note: These suggestions were given to me personally. They are not offered as a roadmap for others but rather as an example of how I was set up to approach my death.*)

In general, the information was delivered in two parts:

1. *Spiritually, my basic daily practice is to deepen my connection to Gourasana and Kalindi.*
2. *Materially, I was given the program on Conscious Departure created in 1996 by a fellow disciple, Vince Roger, M.D. In this program, Dr. Roger says, "The Conscious Departure Program is intended to provide you and your family with a complete and clear summary of all your end-of-life information and advanced planning."*[5]

---

[4] The distinction between 'unworthiness' and 'humility' is explained by Kalindi in her talk "Achieving a State of Full Awareness," 1995, *The Simple Path to God Series*. Feelings of unworthiness can finally end, while "With humility," Kalindi said, "there is always further to go."

[5] In his letter to the Mission, Dr. Roger wrote that as death approaches, the pull of the world intensifies with finances, funeral planning and family responsibilities all requiring more time and attention. This program is designed to help put material life in order so that a conscious decision can be made to spend more of this vital time with God.

Suggestions from The Lady

- *Set up your room conducive to going within.*
- *Address only the most important things.*
- *Be thorough.*
- *When ending separation, your goal is not to make things right, but to leave the other person okay and even feeling empowered.*
- *It is important to complete this pursuit focused on the highest.*
- *Have a tape recorder available so that when realizations and thoughts come up, these can be recorded.*

Dealing with Regrets

- *Choose a confidante to whom you can spew out the garbage. Repeat this "venting" until there is no more life left in these issues. (In this effort, your confidante must be neutral and non-judgmental.)*
- *Perform a thorough cleansing in which you admit regrets and let go of them.*
- *Don't censor anything.*

Dealing with Family

- *Family dynamics become exaggerated as family is left behind.*
- *Often there are more family exchanges at the beginning and fewer later on.*
- *Have an open mind for the process you go through. Do it with great care and integrity.*
- *This business is challenging but not negative.*

The Sacred Passage of the Spirit

- *Feel what it is to be a disciple of Kalindi.*
- *Let go of ideas of what is greeting you.*
- *Be open-minded in this process.*
- *Choose deep music. Often, church music will pull you within.*

- *Develop more trust.*
- *Know that your connection is beyond the mind.*
- *Don't be afraid of what is happening – it's what you do now.*
- *Talk to God.*
- *Be pulled to the power of your words to God.*
- *Go through the eye of the needle, naked.*
- *Feed this desire for the rest of your life.*
- *Kaya will fold into it as you share with her while the process is happening.*

Helping Others

- *You can naturally help others as you go through this period.*
- *Be fueled by your love for humanity.*
- *Know that in this most important time of your life, you are helping to bring in conscious departure.*

At The Lady's suggestion I planned every detail around my dying – from organizing my contact information to the music played at my memorial service. I reviewed and revised my last will and testament, focusing on personal care for my daughter and for the Mission to which I have dedicated my life. I wrote goodbye letters to friends and family and made talks for Kaya to hear each year on her birthday through the age of eighteen.

As I became busy getting my affairs in order, I started putting the material ahead of the spiritual. Even when I realized what was happening, it was hard not to stay captivated by my mind. The difference between what was necessary and what was obsessive was unclear to me. It did not help that I was taking steroids. Steroids produce a horrible and persistent manic drive for perfection. I began relying on new projects to relieve my symptoms. Soon enough I was using material matters to quell panicky feelings.

By the time I began my course of radiation, I was telling myself that my to-do list actually supported my practice to break free. If I desired to be done with this place, I had to get this earthly business off of my plate. On the surface of things, I believed it, even though down deep I knew my spiritual resolve needed to be stronger.

The cover-up worked until I became too uncomfortable not to face the feelings. At that point, I found myself facing a vortex of uncontrollable fear. Even though I didn't want to admit it, I was overwhelmingly afraid of death. This fear was filled with an intensity that ignited my soul. In this state, I faced both the fear and surrender to God's pull to go within. This act of surrender was absolutely necessary to feel the depth of my love for God and His Love for me. And, as the pent-up feelings got released, the mania came under control and the fear dissipated.

A heartfelt moment came when I realized I could love myself even at my worst. I became much kinder and more loving toward my body. I made a personal connection to Gourasana's teaching that whatever happens on this plane of existence – including all atrocities and wars – only increases the love on the spiritual plane. This is a difficult teaching to understand. I found my way to it through Kalindi. She explains that there is a place beneath the pain that is the love. In other words, "The longing *is* the love. It's your love for God, and God's Love for you. It's the thread that pulls you out of material existence back to Him fully."[6]

In my early days on this path I had no concept of my ego and certainly no sense of humility. Back then 'humility' was attached to shame and akin to unworthiness, rather than a doorway to God. It took me years to realize that to be done with unworthiness, I had to turn away from the shame. Only then could I taste true humility.

Death truly is the great equalizer. It allows us to better understand what has value and what does not. With the help of The Lady, my world became

---

[6] The longing is the driving force inside of everyone "that can't be satisfied with anything less than your true beingness in God once again, and your returning back to God." Kalindi's talk, "The Longing Is the Love" (1996) from *The Simple Path to God Series*.

calmer inside and out. I began having quiet early morning meditations that took me deeper and deeper. Having no distractions was a blessing that I would not have seen as such even three to six months before.

Never Underestimate the Power of the Illusion[7]

During the winter of 2010-2011, while undergoing chemotherapy, I began to feel better. After months of physical suffering, I entered a period during which I actually felt okay. I couldn't believe my good fortune. I was filled with so much gratitude just to have a moment's respite from the discomfort in my body. It was delightful to once again feel at ease. I didn't think I'd been healed. I knew it was a phase, part of what happens with cancer. Even so, I felt myself coming back to life. And the world was just outside my door.

By May 2011, my doctor was encouraging me to re-incorporate some physical activities – such as biking and brisk walks – into my schedule. I started online dating. I went off on a long weekend to go skiing, one of my favorite sports since childhood. I still had energy after a day on the slopes and my friends encouraged me by saying, "Wow, you are doing so well!"

Still, some part of me was discontented and I felt depressed. It was all a little bit too much or too little. Something was out of sync. Right about then, The Lady found out about these activities and gave me the following guidance:

> *You are playing with fire. You can't assume anything. . . . You would benefit from saying goodbye to people instead of having excursions with them. Online dating is keeping your material desires in place. Those desires will have you taking [another] birth.*

---

[7] This is one of the principal teachings Gourasana, Kalindi and The Lady have emphasized in their talks and teachings. We must remain vigilant at all times to the illusion's insidious ways and call on God to fill us with His power and presence because "The only way out of the illusion is to fill yourself with the Presence of God." *Let Go, Give Up and Surrender, The Gourasana Sign Book,* (p. 38).

> *You want to advance as far as possible in the precious time you have left. You don't have time to delve into material playtimes.*
>
> *It's the illusory being that doesn't want to die, so it definitely wants you to be interested in online dating and . . . that type of energy. This is opposite of where you need to be going.*

Only after receiving The Lady's guidance did I realize how much I was immersed in material consciousness. I snapped out of it and for a moment felt overwhelmed with shame and guilt. I was being frivolous when there was 'no time to waste.'[8] Then I went within and saw very clearly the illusion delighted in my self-absorption and fed my shame and guilt.

When I looked at my reflection in the mirror, I asked myself, "Who do you think you are?" It was early summer 2011. I'd lost thirteen pounds off an already slight frame. My breasts sagged and my butt drooped. I'd aged ten years in twelve months. One side of my head was scarred, raw and naked. There was an oval of radiated flesh where no hair grew at all. There was not even a hint of my one-time lithe beauty anymore. I'd lost my youthful appearance and good looks, just as now in the spring of 2012, I seem to have found them again, although there is a marked difference in how I see myself. My vanity has disappeared and my focus changed.

Another major aspect of this transition began in August 2011 at the time I was with John of God and ended after the Come into the Light Ashram in September. It started when I came to understand that, though the cancer has been brutal on my body, it has been good for my soul. After that I began to shed habits that had plagued me much of my life. So many of the routines by which I lived out my sense of entitlement and feelings of being worthless simply fell away. It took no effort on my

---

[8] 'No Time to Waste' (1996) is a teaching from Kalindi's talk by that name (*The Simple Path to God Series*). In that talk, she underscores the need for urgency in everyone's spiritual endeavor, whether you want to break free or you just want to evolve and help the world.

part as different social mirrors that once reflected me disappeared. And in this letting go, I found more of myself to love. I relaxed. Peace came over me and, in that blessed moment, I became 'the beautiful gem' that Gourasana speaks about. I could recognize that to be true now.

After that, my course altered. I had always plowed onward in the belief that if I bettered myself, I would be worthy to enter the Kingdom of God. I believed this completely. No matter how many seminars and programs I had done that proved otherwise, I still thought everything was my fault and I deserved to suffer. I had no idea that my beliefs only fortified my being of illusion. Because of unworthiness, I could not believe that God loved me fully and without qualification.

One of the sweetest moments in this time of change came when I heard Kalindi's voice reminding me, "I am a fool. I am lost. I don't know anything." There was such relief in those words for me. Finally, I understood them in my bones. I don't know anything. I control nothing. No matter how clearly I may have seen my life unfolding in a certain way, it is the unexpected that I find everywhere. I did not ask to die, and yet this dying process has become the most significant, eye-opening event of my life.

Although I would not have known how to define the words 'conscious departure' six months ago, I now recognize that my whole life has been lived in order to get to this singular moment and to do it consciously, fully awake and aware.

We live in a time when much is written about death. Elisabeth Kübler-Ross, the Swiss-American scientist, wrote her groundbreaking book *On Death and Dying* in 1969. Her voice was the first to gain prominence by broaching what was then a taboo subject. Today, entire sections of bookstores are devoted to death and dying. There are books about near-death and out-of-body experiences, not to mention miraculous cures and prayer-filled interventions. But I've never come across anything about how to prepare both spiritually and materially for death by letting go of habits, concepts and beliefs in order to break free from the cycle of birth and death.

In Kalindi's talk, "No Concepts at the Time of Death" (1998) from *The Bottom Line Series*, she guides us to become more open-minded as we approach the end of life. Open-mindedness requires giving up any and all ideas about how we think it will be when death arrives. We won't know until it happens. Still, we create pictures and concepts of the moment of death of the body. Kalindi warns us that the more we hold onto these ideas or pictures, the harder it is to completely let go into God. We can't take our concepts with us. We must leave everything behind in the final goodbye.

Saying Goodbyes

As midsummer approached, I set off one Sunday to say goodbye to Christoph, who was once again leaving for Germany. In all likelihood this was our final good-bye. I doubted I would see him again. Even though he and I had broken up several years before, I found this parting to be heart wrenching.

It didn't matter that I'd never experienced what people call 'the greatest love of my life,' at least not with a human being. Still, Christoph was number one for me, and there was something unexpectedly profound about saying goodbye to him now. What I had with him I will never have again. This goodbye represented letting go of illusory love with men and sex, not to mention the role I'd played in all of it.

Christoph invited me to his farewell barbeque at the house of his best friend. Only a few other friends had been invited. As usual, Christoph was cooking. Being side by side again was as natural as it was sweet. The hours passed quickly. When it came time for me to leave, I couldn't stop kissing him. Mine were not erotic kisses. There was no neediness in them. We were no longer lovers but remained good friends. My kisses were for friendship and the love it engenders in me. I feel fortunate to have lived life in company with men like Christoph. I have known such close male friends and now am grateful for both the experience and that I no longer have expectations of them.

Cancer has taught me that there is no future in expectations. Life is not found there. God does not reside there. Nothing lives in expectation except the mind and make-believe. I can't know ahead of time what God has in store for me, but I have learned with absolute certainty that I can trust God's Love.

Final Journey Meditations (1988)

Just as Kalindi said death is the most important event of our lives, Gourasana gave us His "Final Journey Meditations" as a way to prepare for death.[9] By the time I was diagnosed with cancer, the message found on these talks was burned into my soul. Final Journey II (see next section) became the most influential of my life. It is the only talk I plan to listen to at the time of dying.

First, I will share from "Final Journey Meditation I," as described in Gourasana's book *The Radical Path Home to God:*[10]

> *The Final Meditation is significant, because when practicing this meditation with your heart, completely going into your consciousness, you will see what you are hanging on to. You must practice it sincerely. You must not practice it as an intellectual exercise. You must enter completely into the mood as if it is your final meditation and it is time to let go of everything. . . . Because there will come a time when you do the Final Meditation in earnest and you will leave, and if there is still something that you do not want to let go of, then you will again take birth.*
>
> Gourasana, August 20, 1988

---

[9] Two talks by that name were made in 1988, one in August and the other in November. I have listened to the latter discourse almost every night for the past eighteen years. By my calculation, I listened to this meditation more than five thousand times.
[10] Gourasana, *The Radical Path Home to God,* (pp. 346-350).

On "Final Journey Meditation I," Gourasana talks about what it will be like at the end when we are actually dying and there is no more interest in the needs of the body or the mind. This talk has been extremely helpful in my adopting a positive outlook on death. Gourasana suggests in "Final Journey I" that "letting go should be gentle." He promises that there is "nothing to lament" and "no feeling of separation." In fact,

> *All the things that you have been hanging on to have just been suffocating these feelings of love that [we] have been seeking. . . . So while there is still need to let go, you gladly let go because you know that these things are just illusion and they no longer have any meaning. They no longer have any bearing on your existence. And as you leave this body for good, you will be leaving this plane of existence once and for all – for good, never to return.*

He suggests:

> *Feel it, because it is a reality. You will not eat again. You will not sleep again. You will not feel pain again. You will not suffer again. . . . [In this realm] there is nothing but unconditional love.*

He recommends that, as we fall asleep each night, we should focus on this moment as being our final meditation. I have taken His words and this practice to heart.

Final Journey Meditation II

Gourasana recorded a second Final Journey Meditation in November 1988. This is the talk that I'll refer to as 'Final Journey II.' I have fallen asleep to this guided meditation almost every night for the past eighteen years. At some deep level, I have taken in the words Gourasana speaks on a cellular level.

In facing my death, I now know that what I have not learned does not need to be learned. There is nothing more to philosophize about. I let go of who I think I am because everything I identify as 'me' is about to disappear. The resistant, suffering, egotistical me no longer controls the show. I have done enough. It is time to say goodbye to everything, including whatever might still tug at me.

Gourasana instructs those of us seeking to break the cycle of birth and death,

> *If you have the desire to leave, then you will leave. It is so simple. One only returns because they desire to return.*

Kalindi tells us that only those blessed to prepare for final departure ever come in contact with an Incarnation of God. Because of this contact, nothing I do comes with a price too high to pay. It has all been worth it. I have found something rare indeed. And whether or not I attain full union with God, I will go out knowing that I found the Lord in my heart and praying to never feel separate from Him again.

Letting Go of Subtle Attachments

I'm peacefully aware that I will never complete either my material or spiritual to-do lists. Nevertheless, every day now I look at whether or not I'm complete in my incompletion.

This does not mean that I have let go of all my attachments. Rather, it means that incompletion has stopped being so much of a problem. At the end of the day, if I've kept my connection, faced what I had to, and let go of what I could, then there's really nothing left undone.

And speaking of always having something more to let go, just when I was feeling good about my state of letting go, it came over me how much I missed Kalindi in the body. Suddenly, a renewed sense of incompletion overwhelmed me. Without warning, I felt so separated from my spiritual master. This, after I thought I was done with missing her. The sorrow caught me utterly by surprise. I ached for physical contact with Kalindi. I hungered to look into her eyes and breathe in her scent. Being near her had been everything to me. I gained such strength in her presence. I can still hear the sound of her voice and the way she laughed.

And then in my sorrow, I feel her energy inside of me and in all sincerity, know that Kalindi is here. She is alive. She is as she promised she would be – available to everyone in spirit now that she is no longer limited by being in a body. And at the last, Kalindi reminds me that even the feelings I have for my master must be given up if I am going to depart this plane forever.[11]

Love And Ecstasy Beyond Your Comprehension
"The Glory of Change"

---

[11] This Zen Koan is attributed to Master Linji: "If you meet The Buddha on the road, kill him." In other words, if you have any image of enlightenment, it must be thrown out. Nothing and no one can stand between the Source and the soul returning Home.

CHAPTER 13

"It's a Miracle..."

It's been almost two years since I was first diagnosed with a Grade Three brain tumor. From the beginning, the MRIs tell the story in pictures.

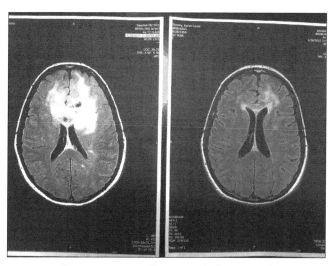

**Comparison of tumor (white area)
from July 29, 2010 to January 23, 2012**

The first picture taken in July 2010 is that of a very large, fast-growing and aggressive malignancy. Between then and the beginning of this year I felt like I was looking down the barrel of a gun. Sometimes I could even feel this living thing growing inside my head.

Now all of that has changed. The last picture taken in January 2012 is of a fading, shadowy tumor. The cancer is practically gone. How that degree of healing happened, I can't say. Nor can I predict if my remission will last. No matter. I feel like I'm living in some kind of miracle within God's destiny for me.

I am one of many cancer patients who have come to see this disease as a blessing in disguise. As horrible as it has been physically and emotionally, I have advanced very fast spiritually as a result of the cancer. Because of the seriousness of my predicament, I came to know what it is not to waste time, as well as how to quickly let go of what no longer serves my highest goal. Whether I live or die, I am now certain that Gourasana is always drawing me closer to my deep desire to break free from this material illusion, just as Kalindi's energy brings me more fully awake and conscious.

Truthfully, I had no inkling that the tumor would go away. I consider it nothing short of a miracle that I am not dead or irreparably brain damaged. As the reader well knows, I have been preparing diligently for death since October 2010. I surrendered to my predicament and a condition that I believed would only get worse.

Recovering from the shock of this change in my prognosis has been easier than weaning myself from Ativan and other highly addictive anti-seizure and sleep medications. The doctors initiated this change immediately after my last MRI in January. Since then I've had to work hard to reduce my intake of drugs. It has been difficult to discern the difference between what I crave and what is necessary. And even though I have done this gradually, the unpleasant side effects of withdrawal have been challenging.

A MAD DESIRE FOR GOD   Chapter 13

Nothing could have prepared me for the physical suffering and mental agitation that comes with withdrawal. For weeks, I had no relief from nausea, headaches and irritability. Simultaneously, I experienced a great deal of stress and even paranoia. Sometimes I had to remind myself that it was the drugs and not me.

Coming off of pharmaceuticals has one sure telltale sign that overwhelms me unless I act immediately. I have to do something whenever I start to feel a sinking depression. Vigorous exercise and dancing are good antidotes, as is any other activity that keeps my mind sharp and my energy flowing. It works best when I don't wait for the symptoms to start. First thing most mornings, I put on a few songs and consciously open up to the energy of God. This helps to clear the cobwebs and both refresh my connection and set my course for the day.

I recently discovered that, because of the tumor's location, my balance and hand-eye coordination (located in left and right hemispheres) have been affected. Yoga is especially helpful. Even when I am utterly clumsy, yoga still bridges the communications gap between these two distinct hemispheres. I am always more grounded after taking yoga. I go to class three times a week. I walk or hike an hour and a half every day. Sometimes my three-year-old Shih Tzu, Bella, comes with me. There are those days when I feel at my worst and Bella is the only reason I get outside in the morning. She and I walk into town or down the swift-flowing, snow-fed creek that cuts through Golden, Colorado. Now more than ever, exercise is essential to the quality of my state of mind and body. While I exercise, if I am not speaking into my recorder, I am praying to God constantly. I pray out loud. Prayer is what keeps me sane and fortifies me as I make this transition from what was to what is.

Fortunately and quite unexpectedly, my short-term memory is returning. I have more of my wits about me, and my mental faculties are sharper now than six months ago. I attribute this improvement in part to how well I take care of my body through diet and exercise. Still, I often feel such waves of fatigue that I need to lie down and close my eyes.

The world may continue to spin around, but lying there I can grow calm inside. At other times, I am filled with so much emotion that all I can do is sit on the floor and scream into a towel or cry. It takes less than a minute for me to let go of excess energy and emotion and grow calm enough to access a depth of longing that brings me to my connection. When times get hardest, I call upon The Lady (the energy of the Mother – her compassion and special mercy) to lift me out of any depression or darkness. When I pray to her, I feel her immediately. She is my lifeboat in the stormiest of seas.

Kaya has had her hard days alongside mine. She was working so hard to prepare for my death. And now, even though my positive prognosis *is* the miracle she prayed for, she displays all kinds of anxiety symptoms, including constant nightmares and obsessive nail biting until the tips of her fingers bleed. It's as if she is experiencing a kind of emotional and psychic whiplash. First, her mom is being taken away and then she is being given back. My illness has had her question whether or not she can trust God, or even if there is a God.

One morning recently, Kaya crawled up next to me in bed and sobbed her eyes out, begging me not to leave her. She kept repeating, "I just don't want to be left alone." Of course, I feel her pain deeply. Hers is a natural reaction. And I believe that what is happening to Kaya is part of her own soul's journey. I play a role, but it is her story. Like me, and all of us, she needs to go through the pain and heartbreak in order to find God's Love. Even as I know I cannot shield her from the pain, I do not want to cause her additional suffering. I never dreamt I would cause my daughter to suffer as she has. And yet I have been the reason for so much. This is God's plan for her and for me. It is His way of getting us to turn toward Him.

Since my remission, Kaya steps further into the stream of life with kids her age. I now know she will be fine no matter what happens. I believe that my greatest responsibility is to leave Kaya standing strong in herself, knowing that she is worthy of God's Love.

Kalindi wanted the children born to her disciples to have a direct experience of the spiritual path their parents chose to walk. Kalindi loved making connection with the younger generations born into this Mission. She wanted the children to be raised with compassion and respect. She did not wish us to push our paths on them, but only to speak words of truth and let them find their own way. She cautioned against spoiling children. When a child is caught up in illusion, she recommended that they meditate and be guided to use the thinking part to examine what lies beneath misbehavior, rudeness or lack of self-worth. She believed that all children should grow up knowing they are beautiful gems with a purpose in God's master plan.

All my relationships have changed. The most miraculous for me is that with my mother. She has become so much sweeter and less charged around me. I am no longer so disturbed when she rants and raves, and so much more accepting. Our hearts have opened to each other. We have found common ground in my writing my story, which included aspects of her life story she could never seem to memorialize. The past has been forgiven if not forgotten. Finally I see my mother's soul as clearly as I feel my own. We are two fragments of God making our way Home to Him eventually.

Recently, The Lady played a talk from Kalindi entitled "Love, Forgiveness, Pain and Compassion." This was recorded on February 25, 2009, shortly before Kalindi left the body. On this talk, she says,

> *In order to move along on this path . . . for growth to happen, harmony to happen, to save ourselves as a human race, there needs to be love and forgiveness. In order for there to be love and forgiveness, there has to be acceptance of pain in the heart. . . . Love and forgiveness are the only reality. . . .*
>
> *Judgment is of the devil. . . . Harmful judgments keep [us] from feeling the love of God. . . . To have the love of God is to have the pain of God [as well as] forgiveness and compassion.*

Kalindi never stopped progressing. She reached greater and greater states of love, compassion and forgiveness. She allowed her heart to be pierced through by the pain endured by humankind. She fully surrendered to God's will and allowed radical change to take place every day in life and body so that she could fulfill her destiny on earth.

Even as she lived so fully and completely, Kalindi talked about dying. When she appeared to be fully alive, she used to say, "I'm dying now." She said it with such certainty that those around her believed it was going to happen that day. She lived in the moment. Then she let the moment go.

By example she showed us that there is always further to go. Kalindi always allowed Gourasana's energy to take her further. And because of her absolute trust and faith in 'The Almighty Supreme,' Kalindi moved faster spiritually than any person I've ever seen. She came to embody the purest love and light I have ever known.

Nobody can travel the same path as Kalindi. Given her special destiny as 'Spiritual Master for This World,' she had to let go, give up and surrender every single second of her existence. This was her path. It is why my story is only one among many that Kalindi's devoted disciples can tell.

Although Kalindi's spirit is no longer housed in a body, she is not gone. Now, she is free to come through all of us. It is my divine duty to represent her to the world in everything I do. Besides breaking free, the greatest gift I can give to Kalindi is to be a living example of her teachings. My greatest desire is to pass these teachings on to others in a personal way, just as Kalindi brought them to me.

From my nineteen years on this Path, I have come to realize that there is nothing to be gained by hanging on and everything to be achieved by dropping the ego in service to the higher good. Gourasana urged those who would listen to follow what became known as 'The Creed':[1]

---

[1] Gourasana, *Breaking the Cycle of Birth & Death,* (p. 89).

Quote #293

> *Become worthy. Become worthy by letting go of your ego. When you feel that power when helping another, rather than thinking that this power is coming from you, say a prayer. If you wish to address that power as the Lord, then you can say, 'Lord, please come through me more and help this person more.' Feel the compassion of the Lord. Feel the love of the Lord. Feel the power of the Lord. Pray that it will increase so that this person can be helped. Pray that you will disappear until it is just the Lord and the person. You become so egoless that who you think you are completely disappears. You become a transparent medium between the Lord and the person. Become worthy and do this.*

Every day, I thank God that I am here to live another day to love and serve Him. What higher goal can one achieve than this?

Dancing in ecstasy, January 2012

CHAPTER 14

Conclusion

A Mad Desire for God has taken me far downstream to all sorts of places I never thought I would visit. I made this journey never knowing what was next or even if I would be given the chance to finish this book. Over my nineteen years on this Path, I have learned that 'With God, all things are possible.' And when I go deep enough into the longing in my heart, I touch God, and that touch keeps me pointed in the direction of greater awareness, more love and more God consciousness in everything I do.

What a miracle it was that Kalindi suddenly appeared in my life. How graced I was to meet a spiritual master powerful enough to break me free. Through the years of my discipleship with her, the cumulative changes I've made have been monumental. After meeting Kalindi, all I wanted was more love and truth in my life. By the time I was diagnosed with cancer, I was forced to face death square on. This diagnosis fully ignited my desire to break free of the cycle of birth and death in this lifetime, and with Kalindi's and The Lady's help, that desire only increases and the prospect of it becomes more real.

As I find my new rhythms, I wonder about the tumor. Will it disappear in time or keep growing? How long will I continue to live from MRI to MRI? One thing is for sure: the cancer has been a place and an experience where enlightenment has become possible.

Over the past year and a half, my illness has become an almost limitless opportunity to discern whether what faces me is real or not. I have learned to live in the present as being the only place where I am truly alive. I have broken through many illusions. Fear, self-importance and vanity no longer govern me. Facing mortality has made living more vibrant and precious. The illusion that I have any control over my death has vanished.

Because of my illness and God's plan for me, more and more of the darkness now yields to the light. And in this greater light, I feel graced by what God makes possible every day, whether it is painful or joyful. All of it fills me with His energy, compassion and desire for my freedom.

For me, the one teaching I return to again and again is that God is my only solace. It is to God that I turn for everything. And in turning to God, I find there is always further into Him to go. No matter what I have achieved spiritually, no matter how far I fall into His arms, there is always a deeper, sweeter, more openhearted love to experience. There is no end or beginning to this love. God's Love is the only constant and it is for everyone unconditionally.

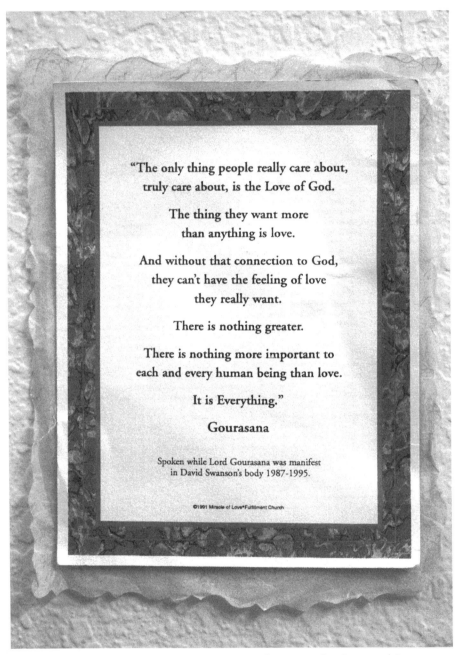

Gourasana's quote on love of God from my bathroom altar

Made in the USA
San Bernardino, CA
02 January 2013